tunisian
CROCHET
encore

**new stitches, new techniques,
new patterns**

Sheryl Thies

Martingale®
Create with Confidence

Dedication: For Jackie, friend and valued advisor

Tunisian Crochet Encore:
New Stitches, New Techniques, New Patterns
© 2013 by By Sheryl Thies

Martingale®
19021 120th Ave. NE, Suite 102
Bothell, WA 98011 USA
ShopMartingale.com

CREDITS
President & CEO: Tom Wierzbicki
Editor in Chief: Mary V. Green
Design Director: Paula Schlosser
Managing Editor: Karen Costello Soltys
Acquisitions Editor: Karen M. Burns
Technical Editor: Ursula Reikes
Copy Editor: Marcy Heffernan
Production Manager: Regina Girard
Cover & Text Designer: Adrienne Smitke
Illustrator: Kathryn Conway
Photographer: Brent Kane

Printed in China
18 17 16 15 14 13   8 7 6 5 4 3 2 1

Mission Statement

Dedicated to providing quality products
and service to inspire creativity.

Library of Congress Cataloging-in-Publication Data is available upon request.

ISBN: 978-1-60468-225-0

Contents

Prelude

You know the phenomenon, when music is stuck in your head and plays over and over again. It might be a simple melody, a snippet of a kids' song with a catchy rhyme, or an advertising jingle with an unforgettable rhythm.

While the actual songs may differ, most of us have had this experience. A recent study discussed at the Society for Consumer Psychology reported that as many as 98% of people have had songs stuck in their heads. This experience is illustrated in animated form in *SpongeBob SquarePants*. There is an episode where SpongeBob can't stop singing a song, annoying everyone at the Krusty Krab.

My theory is that there is something similar occurring with Tunisian crochet. Once people learn the basics, they just can't put their hooks down. Instead, they make project after project after project and can't stop. One student came into the yarn shop, proudly wearing the lovely scarf she'd made in the days immediately following her first class. Another friend is on her 10th afghan and has plans for more. As for myself, I sometimes have to get out of bed in the middle of the night to work up a swatch so that I can go back to sleep without the idea playing over and over again in my head.

My goal for this book was to provide information that will help notch up your confidence and skill level. Tunisian crochet is a wonderful craft with many possibilities, and as your abilities grow, your projects will take on a new level of complexity, and your level of satisfaction with the craft will soar to new heights. Maybe that means more to obsess about; I'm willing to assume that risk and hope you are too.

The first section of this book covers the fundamentals of Tunisian crochet. New techniques and concepts that build on the fundamentals are also presented. Instructions for working short rows to shape and curve edges, double-ended Tunisian crochet to create beautiful reversible fabric, and strategically placed decreases for mitered shapes are all addressed. If you're a true novice who needs more detailed information on the basics, you may want to reference the tutorial in my first book, *Get Hooked on Tunisian Crochet* (Martingale, 2011).

The middle section contains detailed instruction for 16 projects. In addition to the projects that include short rows, double-ended technique, and miters, there are projects made with bulkier yarn and large hooks that work up very quickly. These are as fun to wear as they are to make. The lace projects require a little more patience when working the fine yarn on large hooks, but once done are sure to garner tons of compliments and boost your self-esteem. For a more intricate and unexpected look, there are projects that combine regular crochet with Tunisian crochet. Eye-catching embellishments on many projects intrigue both the crocheter and the wearer.

Useful information on the techniques required for finishing a project, along with helpful resource information, can be found in the "Coda" at the back of the book (page 73).

Each pattern indicates a skill level. The Craft Yarn Council of America provides guidelines for skill levels, but the application of these guidelines is a bit arbitrary. My recommendation is that if you're drawn to the project and comfortable with the very basics, don't get hung up on the skill level; rather, give it a try.

Be creative, express yourself, add your own personal touches, and most of all, take pleasure in the creative process!

~Sheryl

Tunisian Crochet: The Basics

Tunisian crochet produces a richly textured, woven-like fabric. Each row is constructed by making two passes: a forward pass, worked right to left, where stitches are accumulated on the hook; and the return pass, worked left to right, where stitches are worked off the hook. The work is never turned unless the pattern gives specific instructions to do so. For tidy cast-on and bound-off edges, a smaller hook is recommended. The pattern instructions will suggest what hook size to use.

CASTING ON

To create the foundation for Tunisian crochet, make a regular crochet chain. A chain stitch is required for each stitch. You're now ready to begin the foundation row. Both the forward and return passes must be completed for the foundation row.

The foundation pass is worked from right to left into the chain. The first chain stitch from the hook is always skipped; this is the chain stitch already attached to the loop on the hook. Insert the hook into the second chain stitch; yarn over and pull up a loop—two loops on the hook. Insert the hook into the next chain stitch; yarn over and pull up a loop— three loops on the hook. Continue across the row, adding another loop on the hook for each chain stitch worked. Once the last chain stitch is worked, there should be the same number of loops on the hook as there were chain stitches. Never turn the work

unless specifically instructed to do so. When counting stitches, count after completing the forward pass.

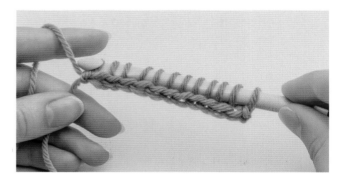

The return pass is worked from left to right as the stitches are worked off the hook. Yarn over and pull through one loop on the hook. The beginning of the return pass is always worked through one loop unless otherwise indicated.

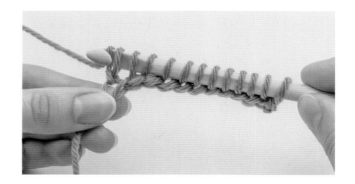

Then *yarn over again and pull through two loops on the hook. Repeat from * across the row until one loop remains on the hook.

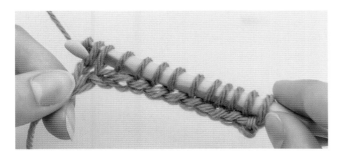

The foundation row is now complete and the one loop remaining on the hook is the start of the next row.

TUNISIAN SIMPLE STITCH (TSS)

Also known as the Afghan stitch, the Tunisian simple stitch is worked in two passes, the forward and the return.

On the forward pass, the first vertical bar below the loop that is already on the hook is always skipped. Insert the hook from right to left behind the front of the next vertical bar between the front and back bars. Yarn over and pull up a loop, keeping it on the hook—two loops are on the hook. Do this behind each vertical bar across the row to the last vertical bar, accumulating loops on the hook as you work to the last stitch.

The last stitch of the forward pass needs a little extra attention to keep the left edge smooth and neat. Insert the hook behind the last vertical bar and the strand that lies directly behind it. To properly identify this strand, look closely, follow this strand upward, and notice that it becomes the lower horizontal strand. With the hook inserted under both these strands, yarn over and pull up the last loop.

Work the return pass the same way as the foundation return pass.

BIND OFF (BO)

A common way to end your work is to bind off using the slip stitch. Other patterns may require a different stitch, which will be stated in the pattern.

At the beginning of the forward pass, *insert the hook behind the next vertical bar, yarn over, and pull through the vertical bar and the loop on the hook—one loop remains on the hook. Repeat from *, working from right to left across the row. Fasten off the last loop.

TUNISIAN KNIT STITCH (TKS)

The Tunisian knit stitch creates a stitch that looks very similar to the knit stitch and is even denser than the simple stitch.

For the forward pass, working from right to left and with the yarn at the back of the work, *insert the hook from front to back between front and back vertical bars and under the horizontal strands, yarn over and pull up a loop. Repeat from * across the row.

The return pass is worked the same as the return pass for the Tunisian simple stitch.

TUNISIAN PURL STITCH (TPS)

At first the Tunisian purl stitch may feel awkward to work, but with some practice, it does become more manageable and comfortable. The stitch is worked with the yarn held in front of the work.

Working from right to left and with the yarn in front, *insert the hook behind the front vertical bar and between the front and back vertical bars as if working the Tunisian simple stitch. Yarn over and pull up a loop. Repeat from * across the row. The return pass is worked the same as the Tunisian simple stitch.

CHANGING COLOR

Color changes can be done at either the left- or the right-hand edge or, for that matter, anywhere within the pattern.

A color change at the right-hand edge is made at the end of the return pass when two loops remain on the hook. Move the color to be dropped to the right, bring the new color to the left and up over the hook, and pull up a loop and pull through both loops on the hook. This locks the new color on the top of the color being dropped, keeping the strand close to the edge. Make the forward pass in the new color.

A color change at the left-hand edge is made after the forward pass is completed. Begin with the first stitch of the return pass. Move the color you're dropping to the left and drop it, bring the new yarn up and over the old yarn, yarn over and pull through one loop, yarn over and pull through two loops; continue with the return pass as usual.

When working in a striped pattern, do NOT cut yarn when the color is changed. Rather, carry the yarn up the side of the work as you go.

When changing color within a row on the forward pass, move the color to be dropped to the left and bring the new color up from behind. For the return pass, when there is one loop of the color to be dropped on the hook and all the other loops are the new color, move the color to be dropped to the right and bring the new color up from behind.

Tunisian Crochet: Beyond the Basics

The various techniques described here will provide a greater range of options for you when shaping and creating your Tunisian fabrics.

DOUBLE-ENDED TUNISIAN CROCHET

Like Tunisian crochet, double-ended Tunisian crochet is also known by a variety of names including "crochenit" and "on-the-double crochet." Worked on a hook with hooks on both ends, the resulting fabric is reversible, and when two different colors are used, each side is usually a different color.

Double-Ended Hooks

Several types of double-ended hooks are available in a range of materials, sizes, and lengths. A double-ended hook can be made any length by purchasing additional hooks for an interchangeable kit and connecting two hooks to the desired length of cord.

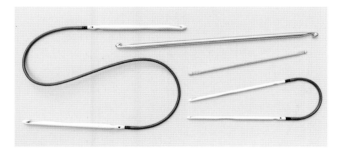

Several types of double-ended hooks

Working Double-Ended Tunisian Crochet

As with regular Tunisian crochet, there is a forward pass where loops are accumulated on the hook, and a return pass where loops are removed from the hook until only one loop remains. A major difference, however, is that the *work is turned*. After the forward pass is completed and all the loops are on the hook, the stitches are slid to the other end and the work is turned before working the return pass. Because the working ball of yarn is now at the opposite end of the hook, the return pass is worked using a different ball of yarn. At the end of the row, when the return pass is completed, the work is not turned and the next row is begun with the forward pass using the same yarn color that was just used for the return pass. Try the following sample to understand how it's done.

1. Chain 12 and work the foundation forward pass as you normally would.

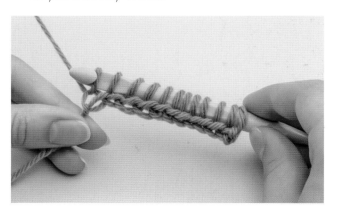

2. Slide the stitches to the other end of the hook and turn the work. Make a slipknot with the second color, place it on the hook, and begin the return pass by pulling the slipknot through the first loop on the hook.

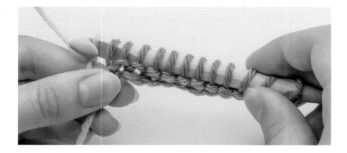

Continue to work the return pass until one loop remains on the hook. Do NOT turn the work.

3. Work the forward pass with the same yarn that was just used for the return pass.

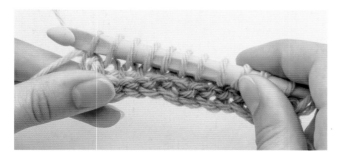

4. Slide the stitches to the other end of the hook, turn, and begin the return pass with different-colored yarn.

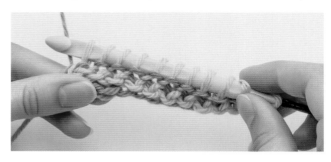

Work a few more forward and return passes so you can see the colors developing on both sides of the swatch.

A strategy for managing your balls of yarn is important to prevent tangling. Turning one way, such as clockwise, and then the other way, counterclockwise, is one such strategy. Or, after completing the turn, moving the balls of yarn to undo any tangles is another. Your specific strategy isn't important, but having one is.

Finding Your Way

Completing a row is always preferable to stopping in the middle, but sometimes life just isn't that simple, and you have to stop wherever you happen to be in order to deal with the situation at hand. When you return to your work, it can be a little confusing to know if you're to work a forward or return pass. Developing a strategy for keeping track of your work when you're not working on the piece is important. My personal strategy is that I place the piece on a table or the floor, directly in front of me, just as I was working on the piece. When I return to my work, I simply pick it up and am ready to continue in the direction I was going before stopping. This strategy may not work for you, especially if you have pets, little kids, or others who share your workspace. Developing your own plan and always putting down your work the same way will help you avoid momentary confusion.

Working with a Short Hook

The actual length of the double-ended hook is not important and is more of a personal preference. It's possible to work a wide afghan with a short double-ended hook. The hook will not accommodate the total number of stitches required, but by working in a series of segments across each pass, the row is completed before beginning the next row.

Work the foundation forward pass until the hook is full, leaving the remainder of the chain stitches unworked, slide the stitches to other end of the hook, and turn. With the second ball of yarn, begin the return pass (yarn over and pull through one loop, *yarn over and pull through two loops, repeat from *). When there are five loops on the hook, slide the stitches to the other end and turn the work. Continue with the foundation forward pass. If the piece is wide and the hook is again filled with loops, slide and turn the work; then continue with the return pass (yarn over and pull through two loops). Continue working the foundation forward and return passes until the end of the row is completed. Remember that you begin the return pass by working a yarn over and pulling through one loop at the beginning of the pass only. Every time you go back and continue your way across the return pass, you *yarn over and pull through two loops, and then repeat from *. Continue with a new row, once again working in steps across each pass.

Working in the Round

Double-ended Tunisian crochet can be joined and worked seamlessly in the round. Again the length of the hook isn't important, as the piece is worked in segments across the passes. A movable stitch marker is used to mark the beginning of a round.

One yarn and one end of the hook can be designated as the forward yarn and hook, while the other ball of yarn and the other end of the hook can be designated as the return yarn and hook. Work the forward pass until the hook is full, then slide and turn the work. Begin the return pass with the second ball of yarn, yarn over, and pull through one loop, *yarn over and pull through two loops; repeat from * until three loops remain on the hook, turn, and continue by making a forward pass. When working the return pass, always continue by making a yarn over and pulling through two loops. Continue alternating between the forward and return passes until the desired length is reached. It will seem as if the return hook and yarn is always chasing or trying to catch up to the forward hook and yarn.

WORKING TUNISIAN SHORT ROWS

The short-row technique provides the subtle shaping of a sloped or curved edge and is helpful when changing the shape of a piece of work without changing the width of the piece.

A short row is simply a row where only a partial number of stitches are worked. This gives the initial appearance of a step. Short rows can be used on either edge of the piece, and any stitch pattern can be used. Often a different stitch pattern is used for the short row to maximize the visual impact.

The first step is to work the designated number of stitches; in the example below, seven stitches are worked in the forward pass. Work the standard return pass (yarn over and pull through one loop, *yarn over and pull through two loops; repeat from *). In other words, the forward and return passes of a short row are worked just like any other row, just not the whole way across.

On the following row, the left-end stitch of the short row needs a little special treatment to minimize a hole appearing in the fabric at the point of the jog. There are two ways of working this stitch, and the pattern will tell you which method works best for a given project. Both methods help soften the slope and lessen the jog that naturally occurs between rows.

Minimizing Holes, Method 1 (2 Strands)

Work the stitches normally up to the last stitch of the short row. Work the last stitch of the short row the same as you would work any left-edge last stitch. Insert the hook behind the vertical bar and the strand that lies directly behind it, yarn over, and pull up a loop.

After working this edge stitch, continue across the row to the end before working the return pass normally.

Minimizing Holes, Method 2 (Slip Stitch)

Work the stitches normally up to the last stitch of the short row. Slip the last stitch of the short row onto the hook before going on to the next stitch. Insert the hook behind the vertical bar and leave it on the hook, without working it. Continue across to the end before working the return pass.

Working Left-Edge Short Rows

A short row can be worked on the left edge of a piece. Complete the forward pass. Work the return pass for the specified number of stitches, leaving the remaining stitches from the previous forward pass on the hook while the next forward pass is worked across to the left edge. Work the return pass as usual.

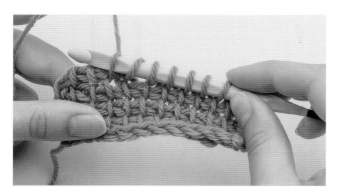

WORKING TUNISIAN MITERS

A miter, worked with a double decrease, changes the shape of the fabric, making a square, diamond, or rectangle shape. With Tunisian crochet, miters are worked over an odd number of stitches with a double decrease generally worked on the return pass. The placement of the decrease depends on the desired shape and will be indicated in the pattern.

To work a double decrease on the return pass, yarn over and pull through four loops on the hook. This creates a cluster of three stitches.

On the forward pass, work a stitch using only the center vertical bar of the three-stitch cluster.

Depending on the configuration of the miters, triangles may be worked at each side edge to provide a straight edge. A triangle requires a single decrease and is worked on the return pass, creating a two-stitch cluster. For a left-edge triangle, the decrease is made at the beginning of the return pass by working a yarn over and pulling through two loops. On the next forward pass, only the outermost stitch of the cluster is worked.

For a right-edge triangle, the decrease is made at the end of the return pass when three loops remain, and the decrease is worked by making a yarn over and pulling through three loops. This, too, causes a two-stitch cluster. On the next forward pass, the cluster is skipped, because the stitch that results from the last stitch of the return pass, which is the decrease, is the first stitch.

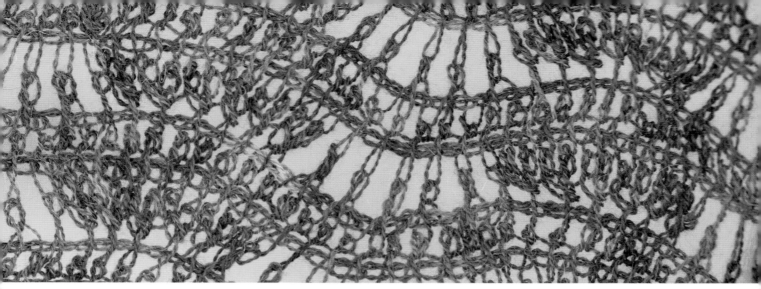

Make It Sing

To help guide the choice of your first project, note the skill-level icon at the beginning of each project, and refer to page 79 for more information regarding skill levels. Even if you're a confident beginner and are drawn to a project that is a higher skill level, don't hesitate to give it a try. All the information you may need to complete the projects is located within this book.

Start by visiting your local yarn shop to select your yarn and needed tools. If you plan on substituting yarn, refer to the yarn-weight chart on page 78 for helpful information. Under the heading of materials, there is a yarn-weight symbol immediately following the yarn used for the project. This will help identify the yarn weight you're looking for. Keep in mind that Tunisian crochet naturally creates a dense, thick fabric, and the projects are worked on a larger hook size than would normally be used for regular crochet.

Before completing your purchase, decide if you want to alter the size of the project. If you want a longer or larger piece, remember to purchase more yarn. The chart on page 78 will help you convert metric measurements.

Be generous with your gauge swatches; consider them an investment toward a successful project. The only way you'll know if you have the right hook size combined with the yarn is to work a swatch. All gauges for the projects are given after blocking. Working the gauge swatch is the perfect way to master your technique, the specific stitch pattern, and suggested finishing. The good news about gauge is that generally row gauge isn't critical because the patterns are written stating the number of inches, rather than number of rows.

You're ready to wind your yarn, pick up your hook, and make it sing.

Ruffled Interlude

Get ruffled and stir things up with this flirty scarf. Short rows create the lavish ruffle flaring along one edge in this easy and quick project. You'll want to make more than one.

SKILL LEVEL

❄ ❄ Easy

FINISHED MEASUREMENTS

Approx 6" x 42"

MATERIALS

One-Color Option

1 skein of Tosh Merino Light from Madelinetosh (100% superwash merino wool; 420 yds/384 m) in color Magnolia Leaf

Two-Color Option

Tough Love Sock from SweetGeorgia Yarns (80% superwash wool, 20% nylon; 4 oz; 425 yds) **1**

A 1 skein in color Bison

B 1 skein in color Violet Hill

For Both

Size J-10 (6 mm) Tunisian crochet hook or size required to obtain gauge

Size I-9 (5.5 mm) crochet hook or one size smaller than hook required for gauge

GAUGE

16 sts = 4" in Tss with larger hook

STITCH GUIDE

Foundation forward pass: *Insert hook in next ch, YO and pull up lp, leave lp on hook; rep from *. Do NOT turn work.

Foundation return pass: YO and pull through 1 lp, *YO and pull through 2 lps; rep from * until 1 lp rem.

Tss forward pass: *Insert hook from right to left behind front vertical bar, YO and pull up lp, leave lp on hook; rep from * across row.

Tss return pass: YO and pull through 1 lp, *YO and pull through 2 lps; rep from * until 1 lp rem.

ExTss forward pass: Ch 1, *insert hook from right to left behind front vertical bar, YO and pull up lp, ch 1, leave lp on hook; rep from * across row.

ExTss return pass: Work as for Tss return pass.

Sc BO: *Insert hook from right to left behind front vertical bar, YO and pull up lp, YO and pull through 2 lps on hook; rep from * until all sts are bound off.

PATTERN

Refer to "Working Tunisian Short Rows" on page 12. Use method 2 to avoid holes.

For 2-color option, work rows 1 and 5 with A, work rows 2, 3, and 4 with B.

Row 1: Work Tss forward and return pass.

Row 2 (short row): Ch 1, ExTss 8, Tss 1 (10 lps on hook). Work Tss return pass.

Row 3 (short row): Ch 1, ExTss 8, slip next vertical bar on hook, ExTss 7, Tss 1 (18 lps on hook). Work Tss return pass.

Row 4 (short row): Ch 1, ExTss 8, Tss 1 (10 lps on hook). Work Tss return pass.

Row 5: Work Tss 8, slip next vertical bar on hook (10 lps on hook), Tss 7, slip next vertical bar on hook (18 lps on hook), Tss 6. Work Tss return pass.

Rep rows 1–5 for patt.

SCARF

With smaller hook, ch 24. Change to Tunisian crochet hook and work foundation forward pass—24 loops on hook. Work return pass.

Beg patt and cont until piece measures 42", ending with row 5. With smaller hook, sc BO. Do NOT cut yarn.

FINISHING

To stabilize neck edge, work crochet edge along non-ruffled straight edge.

Row 1: Sc along long straight edge. Turn work.

Row 2: Ch 1, sc into each sc from previous row.

Weave in all ends. Block using mist method (page 76) to smooth and even out sts.

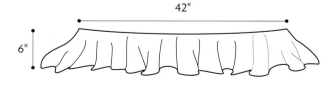

42"

6"

Tempo Primo

This comfortable and casual vest is worked side to side in the simple stitch. To add interest, it's put together so that the wrong side with the subtle slubs is worn as the right side. This is a piece you'll return to time and again as it will help pull together so many great outfits.

SKILL LEVEL

❋ ❋ Easy

SIZES

Finished Bust Measurement: 36 (40, 44, 48)"

Finished Length: 21½ (23¼, 24½, 25½)"

MATERIALS

7 (8, 9, 10) skeins of Tempo by Filatura Di Crosa (51% cotton, 37% acrylic, 12% polyamid; 1.75 oz/50g; 114 yds/105 m) in color 8 Ocean (**4**)

Size K-10½ (6.5 mm) Tunisian crochet hook or size required to obtain gauge

Size J-10 (6 mm) crochet hook or one size smaller than hook required for gauge

GAUGE

13 sts = 4" in Tss with larger hook

STITCH GUIDE

Foundation forward pass: *Insert hook in next ch, YO and pull up lp, leave lp on hook; rep from *. Do NOT turn work.

Foundation return pass: YO and pull through 1 lp, *YO and pull through 2 lps; rep from * until 1 lp rem.

Tss forward pass: *Insert hook from right to left behind front vertical bar, YO and pull up lp, leave lp on hook; rep from * across row.

Tss return pass: YO and pull through 1 lp, *YO and pull through 2 lps; rep from * until 1 lp rem.

Sc BO: *Insert hook from right to left behind front vertical bar, YO and pull up lp, YO and pull through 2 lps on hook; rep from * until sts are bound off.

Sl-st BO: *Insert hook from right to left behind front vertical bar, YO and pull up lp, and pull through 1 lp on hook; rep from * until sts are bound off.

PATTERN NOTES

* *Worked in Tss, but worn with the wrong side facing out.*

* *Worked in one piece from side to side, starting with the left front and ending with the right front.*

LEFT FRONT

With smaller hook, ch 70 (76, 80 83). Change to Tunisian crochet hook. Work foundation forward pass—70 (76, 80 83) lps on hook. Work foundation return pass.

Work in Tss until piece measures 4¼ (5, 5½, 6¼)".

Shape armhole: Sc BO 24 (26, 26, 29) sts, Tss 46 (50, 54, 54). Work return pass.

Work in Tss until armhole measures 3½ (3½, 4, 4)" at end of forward pass.

BACK

Work return pass to end and ch 24 (26, 26, 29).

Work foundation forward pass across 24 (26, 26, 29) chs, Tss 46 (50, 54, 54)—70 (76, 80 83) lps on hook. Work return pass.

Cont in established patt until back measures 14¼ (16½, 18, 20)".

Shape armhole: Sc BO 24 (26, 26, 29) sts, Tss 46 (50, 54, 54).

Work return pass.

Work in Tss until armhole measures 3½ (3½, 4, 4)" at end of forward pass.

RIGHT FRONT

Work return pass to end and ch 24 (26, 26, 29).

Work foundation forward pass across 24 (26, 26, 29) chs, Tss 46 (50, 54, 54)—70 (76, 80 83) lps on hook. Work return pass.

Cont in established patt until right front measures 4¼ (5, 5½, 6¼)".

Neck front: Sc BO 15 sts, Tss 55 (61, 65, 68). Work return pass. Cont in patt until front measures 6 (6½, 7, 7½)" and entire piece measures 36 (40, 44, 48)".

Buttonhole row: Tss 3, (sl-st BO 2 sts, Tss 5) 3 times, Tss across to end. Work return pass, ch 2 over each BO space.

With smaller hook, sc BO.

FINISHING

The bumpy back now becomes the RS. With RS together, sl-st crochet (page 74) shoulder seam.

With smaller hook and bumpy side facing you, sc along all edges, sl st to join, ch 1 and sc into each sc. Position buttons

opposite button holes and sew in place.

Weave in ends. Block using pin-and-mist method (page 76).

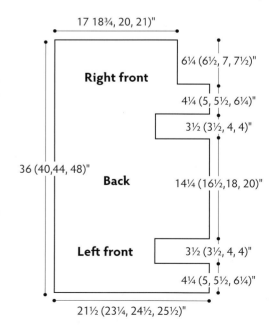

Six-Part Harmony

Six stunning colors, harmoniously arranged in diagonal stripes consisting of diamonds and triangles, make for an easy-to-work and easy-to-wear wrap. No buttonholes are required because the optional button(s) can slip through the double-crochet side edge to provide numerous wearing options.

SKILL LEVEL

Easy

FINISHED MEASUREMENTS

Approx 18" x 45" excluding trim

MATERIALS

Alpaca Silk from Blue Sky Alpacas (50% alpaca, 50% silk; 50 g; 146 yds/133 m) (3)

A 1 skein in color 114 Wisteria

B 1 skein in color 128 Plum

C 1 skein in color 110 Ecru

D 2 skeins in color 100 Slate

E 1 skein in color 115 Oyster

F 1 skein in color 129 Amethyst

Size H-8 (5 mm) Tunisian crochet hook or crochet hook without thumb grip in size required to obtain gauge

1 or more 1"-diameter button(s), optional

GAUGE

1 diamond from point to point = 3"

PROJECT NOTES

- *Refer to "Working Tunisian Miters" on page 13 and read "Mitered Diamonds and Triangles" on page 24 before beginning.*
- *You can use either a Tunisian crochet hook or a standard crochet hook without thumb grip, because the maximum number of stitches on the hook is nine.*
- *Diamond decrease return differs from the standard return pass. The yarn over and pull through four loops is a two-stitch decrease and creates a three-stitch cluster. On the forward pass, only the center stitch of the three-stitch cluster is worked. Refer to the photos on page 13.*
- *Triangle decrease return also differs from the standard return pass. See the right and left triangles. Refer to the photos on page 14.*
- *When picking up loops in adjacent diamonds and triangles, insert the hook through both loops.*

STITCH GUIDE

Foundation forward pass: *Insert hook in next ch, YO and pull up lp, leave lp on hook; rep from *. Do NOT turn work.

Foundation return pass: YO and pull through 1 lp, *YO and pull through 2 lps; rep from * until 1 lp rem.

Tss forward pass: *Insert hook from right to left behind front vertical bar, YO and pull up lp, leave lp on hook; rep from * across row.

Tss return pass: YO and pull through 1 lp, *YO and pull through 2 lps; rep from * until 1 lp rem.

MITERED DIAMONDS AND TRIANGLES

There are two types of diamonds and two types of triangles.

Beginning Diamond

Foundation row: Ch 21, foundation forward pass—21 lps on hook.

Dec return: YO and pull through 1 lp. (YO and pull through 2 lps) 8 times, YO and pull through 4 lps, (YO and pull through 2 lps) 9 times.

Row 1: Tss 8 (9 lps on hook), Tss into central vertical bar of 3-st cluster, Tss 9—19 lps on hook.

Dec return: YO and pull through 1 lp, (YO and pull through 2 lps) 7 times, YO and pull through 4 lps, (YO and pull through 2 lps) 8 times.

Row 2: Tss 7 (8 lps on hook), Tss into central vertical bar of 3-st cluster, Tss 8—17 lps on hook.

Dec return: YO and pull through 1 lp, (YO and pull through 2 lps) 6 times, YO and pull through 4 lps, (YO and pull through 2 lps) 7 times.

Row 3: Tss 6 (7 lps on hook), Tss into central vertical bar of 3-st cluster, Tss 7—15 lps on hook.

Dec return: YO and pull through 1 lp, (YO and pull through 2 lps) 5 times, YO and pull through 4 lps, (YO and pull through 2 lps) 6 times.

Row 4: Tss 5 (6 lps on hook), Tss into central vertical bar of 3-st cluster, Tss 6—13 lps on hook.

Dec return: YO and pull through 1 lp, (YO and pull through 2 lps) 4 times, YO and pull through 4 lps, (YO and pull through 2 lps) 5 times.

Row 5: Tss 4 (5 lps on hook), Tss into central vertical bar of 3-st cluster, Tss 5—11 lps on hook.

Dec return: YO and pull through 1 lp, (YO and pull through 2 lps) 3 times, YO and pull through 4 lps, (YO and pull through 2 lps) 4 times.

Row 6: Tss 3 (4 lps on hook), Tss into central vertical bar of 3-st cluster, Tss 4—9 lps on hook.

Dec return: YO and pull through 1 lp, (YO and pull through 2 lps) 2 times, YO and pull through 4 lps, (YO and pull through 2 lps) 3 times.

Row 7: Tss 2 (3 lps on hook), Tss into central vertical bar of 3-st cluster, Tss 3—7 lps on hook.

Dec return: YO and pull through 1 lp, YO and pull through 2 lps, YO and pull through 4 lps, (YO and pull through 2 lps) 2 times.

Row 8: Tss (2 lps on hook), Tss into central vertical bar of 3-st cluster, Tss 2—5 lps on hook.

Dec return: YO and pull through 1 lp, YO and pull through 4 lps, YO and pull through 2 lps.

Row 9: Tss into central vertical bar of decrease from previous row, Tss—3 lps on hook.

Dec return: YO and pull through 3 lps on hook—1 lp rem on hook.

Do NOT fasten off.

Left-Edge Triangle

Foundation row: (PU lp in each row of previous diamond) 10 times—11 lps on hook. Work dec return pass as follows: YO and pull through 2 lps.

Row 1: Tss 9–10 lps on hook.

Dec return for rows 1–9: *YO and pull through 2 lps; rep from * until 1 lp rem.

Row 2: Tss 8–9 lps on hook.

Row 3: Tss 7–8 lps on hook.

Row 4: Tss 6–7 lps on hook.

Row 5: Tss 5–6 lps on hook.

Row 6: Tss 4–5 lps on hook.

Row 7: Tss 3–4 lps on hook.

Row 8: Tss 2–3 lps on hook.

Row 9: Tss 1–2 lps on hook.

Last dec return: YO and pull through both lps. Cut yarn.

Contiguous Diamonds

Foundation row: (PU lp in each edge of previous diamond) 10 times, (PU lp in each edge of adjacent diamond or triangle) 10 times—21 lps on hook.

Work rows 1–9 as for beg diamond.

Last dec return: YO and pull through 3 lps on hook—1 lp rem on hook.

Right-Edge Triangle

Foundation row: With slipknot on hook, (PU 1 lp in each row of previous diamond) 10 times—11 lps on hook.

Dec return: YO and pull through 1 lp, *YO and pull through 2 lps; rep from * until 3 lps rem, YO and pull through 3 lps.

Row 1: Tss 9—10 lps on hook.

Dec return for rows 1–9: YO and pull through 1 lp, *YO and pull through 2 lps; rep from * until 3 lps rem, YO and pull through 3 lps.

Row 2: Tss 8–9 lps on hook.

Row 3: Tss 7–8 lps on hook.

Row 4: Tss 6–7 lps on hook.

Row 5: Tss 5–6 lps on hook.

Row 6: Tss 5 lps on hook.

Row 7: Tss 3–4 lps on hook.

Row 8: Tss 2–3 lps on hook.

Row 9: Tss 1–2 lps hook.

Last dec return: YO and pull through both lps. Do NOT fasten off.

WRAP

The wrap is worked in diagonal rows.

Row 1: With A, work beg diamond and left triangle.

Row 2: With B, work beg diamond, 2 contiguous diamonds, and left triangle.

Row 3: With C, work beg diamond, 4 contiguous diamonds, and left triangle.

Row 4: With D, work beg diamond, 6 contiguous diamonds, and left triangle.

Row 5: With E, work right triangle, 8 contiguous diamonds, and left triangle.

Row 6: With F, work right triangle, 9 contiguous diamonds, and left triangle.

Row 7: With A, work right triangle, 9 contiguous diamonds, and left triangle.

Row 8: With B, work right triangle, 9 contiguous diamonds, and left triangle.

Row 9: With C, work right triangle, 9 contiguous diamonds, and left triangle.

Row 10: With D, work right triangle, 9 contiguous diamonds, and left triangle.

Row 11: With E, work right triangle, 9 contiguous diamonds, and left triangle.

Row 12: With F, work right triangle, 9 contiguous diamonds, and left triangle.

Row 13: With A, work right triangle, 9 contiguous diamonds, and left triangle.

Row 14: With B, work right triangle, 9 contiguous diamonds, and left triangle.

Row 15: With C, work right triangle and 9 contiguous diamonds.

Row 16: With D, work right triangle and 7 contiguous diamonds.

Row 17: With E, work right triangle and 5 contiguous diamonds.

Row 18: With F, work right triangle and 3 contiguous diamonds.

Row 19: With A, work right triangle and 1 contiguous diamond.

Fasten off.

FINISHING

With RS facing you and D, sc around all 4 sides, working 3 sc into each corner st.

Work crochet trim along each long side edge only as follows.

Row 1: Dc in each st across, turn.

Row 2: Ch 1, sc in each dc across.

Sew button on long side edge near short end if desired.

Weave in all ends. Block using mist method (page 76) to smooth and even out sts.

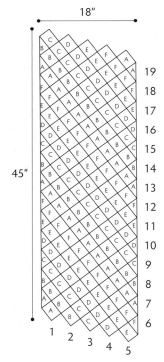

Minuet for Jackie

An impressive shawl-styled jacket that's worthy of its name. Suitable for all three seasons, this garment is worked in a three-row pattern using Tunisian triple-crochet stitches with yarn made from three different fibers. Triple your options by wearing it open, closed, or even upside down with a folded collar.

SKILL LEVEL

✳ ✳ Easy

SIZES

Finished Overall Width: 48 (51, 54)"
Finished Back Width: 14 (15, 16)"
Finished Length: 16¼ (18¼, 20)"

MATERIALS

4 (5, 6) skeins of Lauca from Araucania (80% wool, 10% camel, 10% silk; 100 g; 181 yds) in color 6

Size L-11 (8 mm) Tunisian crochet hook or size required to obtain gauge

Size K-10½ (6.5 mm) crochet hook or one size smaller than Tunisian crochet hook

Shawl pin, optional

GAUGE

12 sts = 4" in patt with larger hook

STITCH GUIDE

Foundation forward pass: *Insert hook in next ch, YO and pull up lp, leave lp on hook; rep from *. Do NOT turn work.

Foundation return pass: YO and pull through 1 lp, *YO and pull through 2 lps; rep from * until 1 lp rem.

Tss forward pass: *Insert hook from right to left behind front vertical bar, YO and pull up lp, leave lp on hook; rep from * across row.

Tss return pass: YO and pull through 1 lp, *YO and pull through 2 lps; rep from * until 1 lp rem.

Tts forward pass: Ch 2, *YO twice, insert hook from right to left behind front vertical bar, YO and pull up lp, (YO and pull through 2 loops) twice, leave lp on hook; rep from * across row.

Tts return pass: Work as for Tss return pass.

Sl-st BO: *Insert hook from right to left behind front vertical bar, YO and pull up lp, and pull through 1 lp on hook; rep from * until sts are bound off.

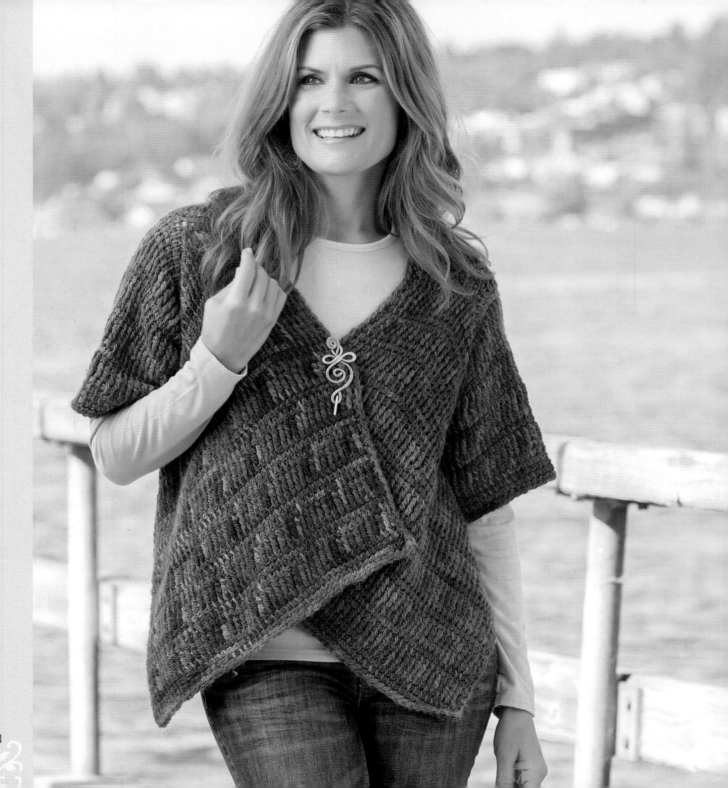

PATTERN STITCH *(ANY NUMBER OF STS)*

Row 1: Tss forward and return pass.

Row 2: Tts forward and return pass.

Row 3: Tss forward and return pass.

Rep rows 1–3 for patt.

PATTERN NOTES

- *Jacket is worked in one piece, beginning with the right front and ending with the left front.*

- *Sleeves are picked up along the armhole edge and worked flat.*

BODY

With smaller hook, ch 49 (55, 61). Change to Tunisian crochet hook. Work foundation forward pass—49 (55, 61) lps on hook. Work foundation return pass.

Work Tss forward and return passes.

Beg patt st and cont until right front measures approx 17 (18, 19)", ending with row 2 return pass.

Shape armhole forward pass:
Work Tss until 12 (13, 14) lps on hook, sl-st BO 21 (24, 27) sts, Tss to end of row—12 (13, 14) lps on hook, BO space, and 16 (18, 20) lps on hook.

Shape armhole return pass: Tss return pass to BO space, chain 21 (24, 27), cont with Tss return pass.

Work row 1 of patt to new chs, work foundation forward pass into each ch, cont with patt across row. Cont in patt until back measures approx 14 (15, 16)" from armhole opening, ending with row 2.

Shape armhole as before.

Cont in patt st until left front measures 17 (18, 19)" from second armhole opening.

Work Tss forward and return passes.

With smaller hook, sl-st BO. Do NOT cut yarn.

Sc along all edges, working 3 sc into each corner. Fasten off and join with duplicate st (page 73).

SLEEVE (MAKE 2.)

With RS facing you and larger hook, beg at underarm, work foundation forward pass to PU 46 (52, 58) sts around armhole opening—46 (52, 58) lps on hook. Work return pass.

Work Tss forward and return passes.

Work patt st for a total of 12 rows, ending with row 3 return pass.

Work 2 rows of Tss forward and return passes.

With smaller hook, sl-st BO.

Rep for other sleeve.

FINISHING

Sl-st crochet (page 74) sleeve underarm. Sc along bottom sleeve edge. Weave in all ends. Block using mist method (page 76) to smooth and even out sts.

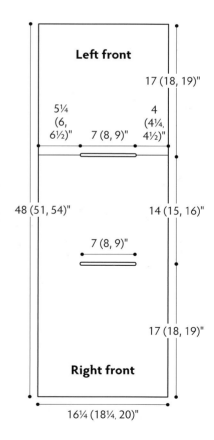

Ruby-Slippers Ballet

A thoroughly modern take on the poncho, this luscious garment is worked in luxurious fibers. Rows of Tunisian simple stitch separate the rows of crochet stars, and the entire piece is tipped with a delicate crocheted picot edge, making this one of the most flattering toppers you'll ever own.

SKILL LEVEL

❋ ❋ Easy

FINISHED MEASUREMENTS

Approx 30" x 34" excluding crochet edge

MATERIALS

3 skeins of Silk/Cashmere from Jade Sapphire Exotic Fibres (55% silk, 45% cashmere; 55g; 400 yds) in color Ruby Slippers #11

Size K-10½ (6.5 mm) Tunisian crochet hook or size required to obtain gauge

Size I-9 (5.5 mm) crochet hook or one size smaller than Tunisian crochet hook

GAUGE

17 sts = 4" in Tss with larger hook

STITCH GUIDE

Foundation forward pass: *Insert hook in next ch, YO, pull up lp and leave lp on hook; rep from *. Do NOT turn work.

Foundation return pass: YO, pull through 1 lp, *YO and pull through 2 lps; rep from * until 1 lp rem.

Tss forward pass: *Insert hook from right to left behind front vertical bar, YO and pull up lp, leave lp on hook: rep from * across row.

Tss return pass: YO and pull through 1 lp, *YO and pull through 2 lps; rep from * across row until 1 lp rem.

Sc BO: *Insert hook from right to left behind front vertical bar, YO and pull up 1 lp, YO and pull though 2 lps; rep from * until sts are bound off.

STAR PATTERN *(MULTIPLE OF 2 STS)*

Row 1: On first row of piece only, foundation forward pass into each ch; on subsequent rows, work foundation forward pass under 2 lps of crochet sts from previous row—72 lps on hook. Work foundation return pass.

Rows 2 and 3 (Tunisian crochet): Tss forward and return passes.

PONCHO (MAKE 2 PIECES.)

With smaller hook, ch 72. Change to Tunisian crochet hook. Work star patt until piece measures 30", ending with row 2 return pass.

With smaller hook, sc BO.

FINISHING

Block both pieces using mist method (page 76).

For neck, measure and place markers 9½" from CO and BO edge. See schematic for layout. With RS together, sl-st crochet (page 74) seam from edge to marker. Repeat for other side.

With RS facing you and smaller hook, sc around neck edge.

Work crochet border around outer edge as follows:

Rnd 1: Sc around entire edge, working 3 sc into each corner st, sl st to join.

Rnd 2: Ch 1, sk first sc, *ch 3, sl st into first ch, sk 1 sc, sc in next sc; rep from * to end, sl st to join. Work sc into each corner st, skipping an extra st if necessary.

Row 4 (regular crochet) (RS):

Ch 2, pick up lp in second ch from hook; starting with first vertical bar below first loop, pick up lp in each of 3 vertical bars (5 lps on hook), YO and pull through 5 lps, ch 1 to create eye of star, *pick up lp in center of eye, pick up lp in back of last lp of star, and pick up lp in each of next 2 vertical bars (5 lps on hook), YO and pull through 5 lps, ch 1; rep from * across row to last st, sc in last st. Turn.

Row 5 (regular crochet) (WS):

Ch 1, sc in first st, 2 hdc into each eye across row, sc in last st. Turn.

Rep rows 1–5 for patt.

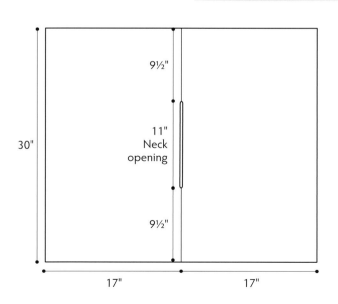

2012 Overture

Oh the fun you can have with your own overture; make a grand entrance and, once the curtain rises, sit back and relish the warmth. Add a stickpin and this quick-to-work-up, over-the-shoulder garment will stay in place, leaving your hands free.

SKILL LEVEL

※ ※ Easy

FINISHED MEASUREMENTS

Approx 20" x 64" (22" x 69")

MATERIALS

Lanaloft Bulky from Brown Sheep Company, Inc. (100% wool; 7 oz; 160 yds/146 m)

A 3 (4) skeins in color 777 Autumn Run

B 1 skein in color 225 Rose Marquee

Size O-17 (12 mm) Tunisian crochet hook or size required to achieve gauge

Size N/P-15 (10 mm) crochet hook or one size smaller than Tunisian crochet hook

GAUGE

8 sts = 4" in ExTss with larger hook

STITCH GUIDE

Foundation forward pass: *Insert hook in next ch, YO, pull up lp and leave lp on hook; rep from *. Do NOT turn work.

Foundation return pass: With B, YO, pull through 1 lp, (YO and pull through 2 lps) 4 times, change to B and *YO and pull through 2 lps; rep from * until 1 lp rem.

ExTss forward pass: With A, ch 1, *insert hook from right to left behind front vertical bar, YO and pull up lp, ch 1, leave lp on hook; rep from * across row.

ExTss return pass: YO and pull through 1 lp, *YO and pull through 2 lps; rep from * across row until 1 lp rem.

Sc BO: *Insert hook from right to left behind front vertical bar, YO and pull up 1 lp, YO and pull through 2 lps; rep from * until all sts are bound off.

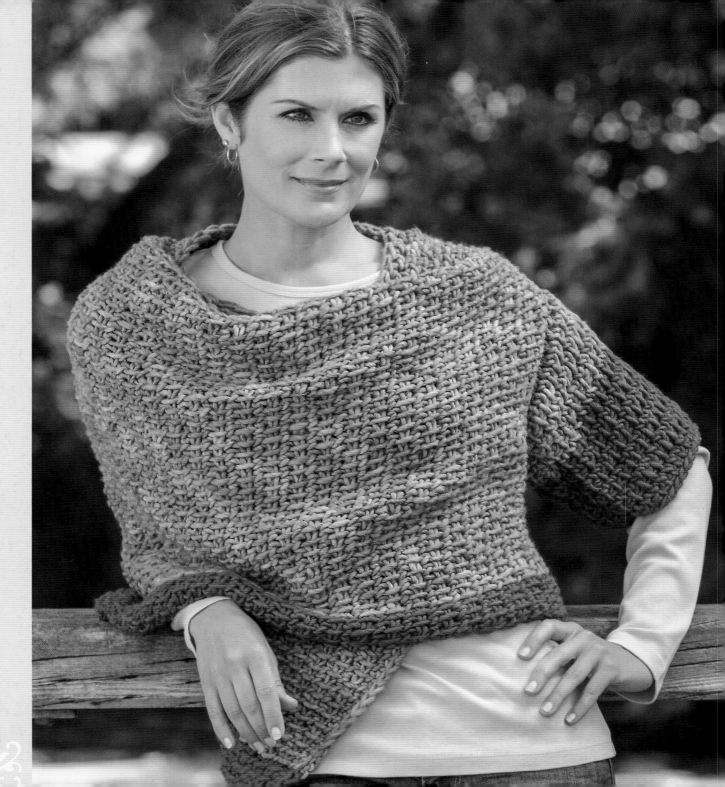

PROJECT NOTES

* *Body is worked in one piece, starting with the right front and ending with the left front.*

* *See "Changing Color" on page 8.*

RIGHT FRONT

With smaller hook and B, ch 5, change to A and ch 35 (39)—40 (44) total chs.

Switch to Tunisian crochet hook. With A, work foundation forward pass until 35 (39) lps on hook, change to B and work foundation forward on last 5 ch—40 (44) lps on hook. Work foundation return pass.

Work in ExTss forward and return passes maintaining color patt until piece measures 15 (17)".

Shape armhole forward pass:
Cont in patt, work 10 lps on hook, BO 16 (18) sts, cont across row in pattern—10 lps on hook, BO space, 14 (16 lps) on hook.

Shape armhole return pass:
Work ExTss return pass to BO space, ch 16 (18), cont with return pass until 1 lp rem.

BACK

Cont in color patt, work ExTss to ch, work foundation forward pass into each ch, cont across row in patt—40 (44) lps on hook. Work return pass.

Cont in patt until back measures 14 (15)".

Shape armhole as before.

LEFT FRONT

Cont in color patt, work ExTss to ch, work foundation forward pass into each ch, cont across row in patt—40 (44) lps on hook. Work return pass.

Cont in patt until left front measures 35 (37)".

With smaller hook, sc BO.

SLEEVE (MAKE 1.)

With B, ch 34 (38).

Cont with B and work 5 rows in ExTss.

Change to A at right edge when 2 lps rem on hook. Cont in ExTss until piece measures 9 (10)".

With smaller hook, sc BO.

FINISHING

Sl-st crochet (page 74) sleeve into left armhole and sleeve underarm.

With smaller hook, RS facing you, and A, beg at underarm, sc along right armhole edge. With RS facing you and A, sc along front edge, changing to B for last 5 sts. Repeat for other front edge, reversing color.

Weave in ends. Block using mist method (page 76).

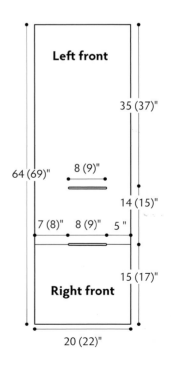

Beaded Trill

Can't decide between a cowl or a scarf? Have it both ways. This versatile, wavy-edged piece, worked in yarn with incredible drape and embellished with beads, provides a showy finish to any attire. With just enough beads to catch the light but not so many that it's weighted down, this piece can be rearranged from scarf to cowl and back again in seconds.

SKILL LEVEL

Intermediate

FINISHED MEASUREMENTS

Approx 5" (at widest point) x 46"

MATERIALS

2 skeins of New York 200 from Interlacements (100% rayon ribbon; 200 yds) in color Wagon Wheel Gap (3)

1 bag pre-strung size #6 glass beads from Interlacements in color Root Beer

OR 520 unstrung size #6 beads

Size K-10½ (6.5 mm) Tunisian crochet hook or size required to obtain gauge

Size I-9 (5.5 mm) crochet hook or one size smaller than Tunisian crochet hook

3 small safety pins (optional)

GAUGE

19 sts = 4" in Tss with larger hook

STITCH GUIDE

Foundation forward pass: *Insert hook in next ch, YO and pull up lp, leave lp on hook; rep from *. Do NOT turn work.

Foundation return pass: YO and pull through 1 lp, *YO and pull through 2 lps; rep from * until 1 lp rem.

Tss forward pass: *Insert hook from right to left behind front vertical bar, YO and pull up lp, leave lp on hook; rep from * across row.

Tss return pass: YO and pull through 1 lp, *YO and pull through 2 lps; rep from * until 1 lp rem.

Tss2tog: Insert hook behind 2 vertical bars, YO and pull up lp.

Beaded sl-st BO: *Insert hook from right to left behind front vertical bar, slide bead up against hook, YO and pull up lp and bead, pulling through lp on hook; rep from * until all sts are bound off.

Sc BO: *Insert hook from right to left behind front vertical bar, YO and pull up 1 lp, YO and pull though 2 lps on hook; rep from * until sts are bound off.

Place bead: Insert hook from right to left behind front vertical bar, slide bead up against hook, YO and pull up lp with bead, leave lp on hook.

PATTERN

Row 1: Tss 2, YO, Tss2tog, YO, Tss 3, place bead, (Tss, place bead) twice, Tss 6—20 lps on hook. Work return pass.

Row 2: Tss 2, YO, Tss2tog, YO, Tss 3, place bead, (Tss, place bead) twice, Tss 7—21 lps on hook. Work return pass.

Row 3: Tss 2, YO, Tss2tog, YO, Tss 3, place bead, (Tss, place bead) twice, Tss 8—22 lps on hook. Work return pass.

Row 4: Tss 2, YO, Tss2tog, YO, Tss 3, place bead, (Tss, place bead) twice, Tss 9—23 lps on hook. Work return pass.

Row 5: Tss 2, YO, Tss2tog, YO, Tss 3, place bead, (Tss, place bead) twice, Tss 10—24 lps on hook. Work return pass.

Row 6: Beaded sl-st BO 5, Tss across—19 lps on hook. Work return pass.

Rep rows 1–6 for patt.

Stringing Beads

You can work with either pre-strung or loose (unstrung) beads.

Pre-strung beads: Beads that are pre-strung on string can easily be moved to the yarn. Very carefully separate the bead strings and tape each end of string to a flat surface such as a countertop or table. Tie the end of the string around one end of the yarn and gently remove the tape. Working with a few beads at a time, slide them over the knot, tugging gently as needed to move them onto the yarn. Once on the yarn, gently slide them back toward the yarn ball to make room for more beads. Once all the beads are off the string and onto the yarn, remove the string.

Loose beads: To string loose beads onto yarn, purchase a big-eye beading needle, usually available at craft stores or wherever beads are sold. Thread the yarn through the eye of the needle, thread the needle tip through a few beads, and slide the beads, tugging gently as necessary to move the bead off the needle and onto the yarn.

Working with beads: I used a total of 520 beads. However, not all the beads need to be strung at one time. String some of the beads and work until the yarn is out of beads. Cut the yarn and string some more beads before continuing. This will create less wear on the yarn, although you'll have a few more ends to weave in.

Place bead.

PROJECTS NOTES

* *Once a bead is placed, it will rest on the front vertical bar. When working the return pass, keep the bead on the front vertical bar and if it slides to the back, move it forward.*

* *Stitch count changes with each row.*

* *Either a Tunisian crochet hook or standard crochet hook without thumb grip can be used because the maximum number of stitches on the hook is 24.*

SCARF

With smaller hook, ch 19. Change to Tunisian crochet hook and work foundation forward pass—19 lps on hook. Work foundation return pass.

Work in patt until piece measures approximately 46", ending with row 6 return pass.

With smaller hook, sc BO.

FINISHING

With RS facing you and smaller hook, beg at CO edge, sc along CO edge, long side and BO edge, working 3 sc into each corner st. Do NOT turn.

With RS still facing you, work in the opposite direction from left to right as follows: ch 1, *rev sc (page 76), ch 1, sk next st; rep from * to beg, sl st to join and fasten off.

To wear as a cowl, pin short edges tog on WS using 3 small safety pins. Or if you want, sew short ends together.

46"

5"

Hummingbird Rhapsody

This generously sized shrug jacket offers fashionable warmth and comfort. The simple design, with vertical rib pattern and circular trim, creates striking lines that will flatter any body shape.

SKILL LEVEL

Intermediate

FINISHED MEASUREMENTS

Approx 41" x 26" (43" x 28", 49" x 30") before folding, excluding circular trim

MATERIALS

3 (3, 4 skeins) of Merino Ribbon from Mountain Colors (80% super fine merino wool, 20% nylon; 100 g; 245 yds) in color Hummingbird (4)

Size N/P-15 (10 mm) Tunisian crochet hook or size required to obtain gauge

Size N/P-15 (10 mm) double-ended Tunisian crochet hook

Size M/N-13 (9 mm) crochet hook or one size smaller than Tunisian crochet hook

Removable stitch marker

GAUGE

10 sts = 5" (Note: this is not the standard 4" gauge swatch; stitches are measured over 5".)

STITCH GUIDE

Foundation forward pass: *Insert hook in next ch, YO and pull up lp, leave lp on hook; rep from *. Do NOT turn work.

Foundation return pass: YO and pull through 1 lp, *YO and pull through 2 lps; rep from * until 1 lp rem.

Tks forward pass: *Insert hook from front to back between front and back vertical bars and under horizontal strands, YO and pull up lp, leave lp on hook; rep from * across row.

Tks return pass: YO and pull through 1 lp, *YO and pull through 2 lps; rep from * until 1 lp rem.

Tks BO: *Insert hook from front to back between front and back vertical bars and under horizontal strands, YO and pull up 1 lp, YO and pull through 2 lps; rep from * until all sts are bound off.

Double-ended ExTks forward pass: *Insert hook from front to back between front and back vertical bars and under horizontal strands, YO and pull up lp, ch 1, leave lp on hook; rep from * across row.

Double-ended ExTks return pass: YO and pull through 1 lp, *YO and pull through 2 lps; rep from * until end. Note the YO and pull through 1 lp occurs only once, and then since the return is worked as a spiral, the return is always YO and pull through 2 lps.

ExTks BO: *Insert hook from front to back between front and back vertical bars and under horizontal strands, YO and pull up 1 lp, YO and pull through 2 lps on hook; rep from * until all sts are bound off.

CROSSED-STITCH RIB PATTERN (MULTIPLE OF 5 STS + 8 STS)

Crossed sts appear on the row below the row being worked.

All rows: Tks 2, *sk next vertical bar, Tss into next vertical bar, Tss into skipped vertical bar, Tks 3; rep from * to last 5 sts, sk next vertical bar, Tss into next vertical bar, Tss into skipped vertical bar, Tks 2, Tss. Work return pass.

PATTERN NOTES

⌘ *The piece is worked in a rectangle, and then folded in half and seamed along the short ends, leaving an opening for the armholes.*

⌘ *The edging is worked along the cast-on and bound-off edges.*

⌘ *To wear, slip each arm into an armhole and pull the jacket around your body. Fold back the edging to create a collar.*

SHRUG

With smaller hook, ch 98 (103, 118) sts. Change to Tunisian crochet hook and work foundation forward pass—98 (103, 118) lps on hook. Work foundation return pass.

Work in patt until piece measures 26 (28, 30)".

With smaller hook, sc BO.

FINISHING

Fold piece in half, WS tog, by bringing CO and BO edges together. Measure 7½ (8, 9)" down from fold on each end and place marker for armhole. Sl-st crochet (page 74) side seam from marker to CO/BO edges.

See "Double-Ended Tunisian Crochet" on page 9. Prepare 2 balls of yarn. Mark beg st with removable marker. With double-ended crochet hook and RS facing you, work foundation forward pass under both strands of each st along CO and BO edges; the exact number does not matter.

Using double-ended crochet hook, work ExTks forward and return passes until edge measures approx 3". Cont with larger hook, ExTks BO.

With smaller hook and RS facing you, sc around armhole edges.

❈ Working Double-Ended Crochet in the Round

Even though the double-ended edge is worked in only one color, there will be one ball of yarn for the forward pass and a second ball of yarn for the return pass. The return-pass ball of yarn will always be following or "chasing" the forward-pass ball.

Work the foundation forward pass about halfway around, turn work, and with second ball of yarn, beg the return pass. Cont with the return pass until roughly 5 lps rem on hook. Turn work and cont with foundation forward pass to marked st. At marked st, beg patt st. Cont working forward and return passes until desired measurement is reached. Be sure to work return pass to marked st before beg BO.

Kimono Concerto

Be the center of attention in this exquisite kimono-styled jacket. The wide three-quarter length sleeves worked from cuff to center back are woven together with bias-cut silk ribbon. The detailed diamond pattern and attractive lacing provide an artistic touch to a captivating piece.

SKILL LEVEL

✵ ✵ ✵ Intermediate

FINISHED MEASUREMENTS

Approx 39" x 45" after lacing

MATERIALS

4 skeins of Scrumptious from Lantern Moon (45% silk, 55% superwash merino; 100g; 399 yds/365 m) in color Oyster

Size K-10½ (6.5 mm) Tunisian crochet hook or size required to obtain gauge

Size J-10 (6 mm) crochet hook or one size smaller than Tunisian crochet hook

5 yds of 1½"-wide Hanah Silk Ribbon from Artemis (100% silk ribbon) in color Old Ivory

GAUGE

15 sts = 4" in patt with larger hook

STITCH GUIDE

Foundation forward pass: *Insert hook in next ch, YO and pull up lp, leave lp on hook; rep from *. Do NOT turn work.

Foundation return pass: YO and pull through 1 lp, *YO and pull through 2 lps; rep from * until 1 lp rem.

Tss forward pass: *Insert hook from right to left behind front vertical bar, YO and pull up lp, leave lp on hook; rep from * across row.

Tss return pass: YO and pull through 1 lp, *YO and pull through 2 lps; rep from * until 1 lp rem.

Sc BO: *Insert hook from right to left behind front vertical bar, YO and pull up 1 lp, YO and pull though 2 lps on hook; rep from * until sts are bound off.

PATTERN
(MULTIPLE OF 12 STS + 4 STS)

YO from previous row appears as a slant rather than vertical bar and is worked as a stitch.

Row 1: Tss, *Tss 5, Tss2tog, YO, Tss 5; rep from * to last 2 vertical bars, Tss 2. Work return pass.

Row 2: Tss, *Tss 4, (Tss2tog, YO) twice, Tss 4; rep from * to last 2 vertical bars, Tss 2. Work return pass.

Row 3: Tss, *Tss 3, (Tss2tog, YO) 3 times, Tss 3; rep from * to last 2 vertical bars, Tss 2. Work return pass.

Row 4: Tss, *Tss 2, (Tss2tog, YO) 4 times, Tss 2; rep from * to last 2 vertical bars, Tss 2. Work return pass.

Row 5: Tss, *Tss 1, (Tss2tog, YO) 5 times, Tss 1; rep from * to last 2 vertical bars, Tss 2. Work return pass.

Row 6: Tss, *Tss 2, (Tss2tog, YO) 4 times, Tss 2; rep from * to last 2 vertical bars, Tss 2. Work return pass.

Row 7: Tss, *Tss 3, (Tss2tog, YO) 3 times, Tss 3; rep from * to last 2 vertical bars, Tss 2. Work return pass.

Row 8: Tss, *Tss 4, (Tss2tog, YO) 2 times, Tss 4; rep from * to last 2 vertical bars, Tss 2. Work return pass.

Rep rows 1–8 for patt.

KIMONO (MAKE 2 PIECES.)

The CO edge will become the center front/back of garment. You'll be working outward to sleeve edge.

With smaller hook, ch 148. Change to Tunisian crochet hook and work foundation forward pass—148 loops on hook. Work return pass.

Work 2 rows Tss forward and return passes.

Work patt until piece measures approx 21", ending with row 1 return pass.

Work 2 rows Tss forward and return passes.

With smaller hook, sc BO. Do NOT cut yarn, turn.

Work crochet edge for lacing eyelets as follows:

Row 1: Ch 1, sc in each st, turn.

Row 2: Ch 2, dc 2, *ch 1, sk next st, dc 3; rep from * to end, turn.

Design Options

Work the crochet eyelet edge along the cast-on edges and weave the silk ribbon for a more embellished cuff edge. Additional silk ribbon will need to be purchased. Or for long sleeves, work two additional pattern repeats on each piece and increase the underarm seam to 14". One additional skein of yarn will need to be purchased.

Row 3: Sl st in each st. Fasten off and cut yarn

FINISHING

Block using mist method (page 76) to smooth and even out sts.

Fold piece in half with RS together by bringing edges together. Place a marker 10" from CO edge, and sl-st crochet (page 74) the seam. Repeat with other piece.

Lay pieces side by side with eyelet edges almost touching. Count 18 eyelets from bottom edge and place marker. Rep for other piece. Fold ribbon in half and working

Ladder Lacing

Mark 18 eyelets up from bottom edge. Fold ribbon in half by bringing the two cut ends together; mark the midpoint.

1. Start each side of ribbon from wrong side and feed it up through bottom eyelet to right side.

2. Take each ribbon straight up on outside of piece and into next eyelet.

3. Cross ribbons and feed under vertical bar just made. Adjust tightness of ribbon.

Rep steps 2 and 3 until 18 sets of eyelets have been laced. Knot ribbon to secure. Feed remaining ribbon over and under front eyelets to last eyelet. Loop remaining ribbon under last vertical bar to secure. Cut remaining ribbon length if desired.

on RS, beg at bottom eyelet, lace ribbon using ladder-lacing method (at left).

With RS facing you and smaller hook, beg at underarm seam and work 3 rows of sc around each sleeve opening. With RS facing you, work 3 rows of sc along bottom edge from front opening to back opening. Mist crochet edge lightly.

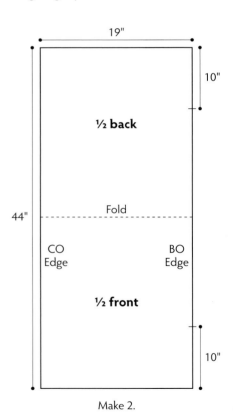

Make 2.

Fan Dance

Light and airy, delicate as a feather, soft as a cloud, and so pretty, this showstopper adds color and style to any outfit. Let these delicate fans dance playfully across your shoulders. Loop it casually over a jacket or T-shirt, or drape it like a shawl.

SKILL LEVEL

※ ※ ※ Intermediate

FINISHED MEASUREMENTS

Approx 13" x 70"

MATERIALS

1 skein of Hand Paint Lace from Misti Alpaca (100% baby alpaca; 100g; 874 yds/800 m) in color 01 Blues in the Night ()

Size J-10 (6 mm) Tunisian crochet hook or size required to obtain gauge

Size I-9 (5.5 mm) crochet hook or one size smaller than Tunisian crochet hook

GAUGE

18 sts = 4" in patt with larger hook

STITCH GUIDE

Foundation forward pass: *Insert hook in next ch, YO and pull up lp, leave lp on hook; rep from *. Do NOT turn work.

Foundation return pass: YO and pull through 1 lp, *YO and pull through 2 lps; rep from * until 1 lp rem.

Tss forward pass: *Insert hook from right to left behind front vertical bar, YO and pull up lp, leave lp on hook; rep from * across row.

Tss return pass: YO and pull through 1 lp, *YO and pull through 2 lps; rep from * until 1 lp rem.

Tdc forward pass: *YO, insert hook from right to left behind front vertical bar, YO and pull up lp, YO and pull through 2 lps, leave lp on hook; rep from * across row.

Tdc return pass: Work as for Tss return pass.

Tdc2tog: (YO and pull up lp, YO and pull through 2 lps) in each of the next two sts, YO and pull through 2 lps.

Sc BO: *Insert hook from right to left behind front vertical bar, YO and pull up lp, YO and pull though 2 lps on hook; rep from * until all sts are bound off.

FEATHER FAN STITCH
(MULTIPLE OF 18 STS + 22 STS)

YO from previous row appears as a slant rather than vertical bar and is worked as a stitch.

Two YOs will be made in a row when working the "YO, Tdc" sts, one for the YO and one for the Tdc.

Row 1: Ch 2, Tdc, (Tdc2tog in next 2 sts) 3 times, *(YO, Tdc) 6 times, (Tdc2tog in next 2 sts) 6 times; rep from * to last 14 sts, (YO, Tdc) 6 times, (Tdc2tog in next 2 sts) 3 times, Tdc 2. Work return pass.

Row 2: Ch 2, *Tdc; rep from * across. Work return pass.

Rep rows 1 and 2 for patt.

SCARF

With smaller hook, ch 58. Change to Tunisian crochet hook and work foundation forward pass—58 lps on hook. Work foundation return pass.

Ch 2 and work Tdc forward and return passes.

Work feather fan st until piece measures approx 70", ending with row 2 return pass.

With smaller hook, sc BO.

FINISHING

Weave in all ends. Block using mist method (page 76) to smooth and even out sts.

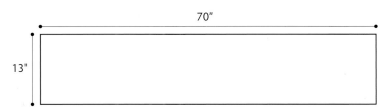

70"

13"

Counterpoint

Toss this versatile, oversized Mobius cowl over anything—from T-shirts to sweaters to dresses—for a stylish boutique look. The subtle contrast of the colorplay, the open-work stitches, and the comfortable fit provide a lightweight, year-round accessory.

SKILL LEVEL

✺ ✺ ✺ Intermediate

FINISHED MEASUREMENTS

Approx 21" x 60"

MATERIALS

Soft Linen from Classic Elite Yarns (35% wool, 35% linen, 30% baby alpaca; 50 g; 137 yds)

A 3 skeins in color 2204 Titian Blue

B 3 skeins in color 2248 Blue Grotto

Size N/P-15 (10 mm) double-ended Tunisian crochet hook or size required to obtain gauge

Size M/N-13 (9 mm) crochet hook or one size smaller than Tunisian crochet hook

GAUGE

11 sts = 4" in patt with larger hook

STITCH GUIDE

Foundation forward pass: *Insert hook in next ch, YO and pull up lp, leave lp on hook; rep from *. Do NOT turn work.

Double-ended foundation return pass: Turn and slide sts to other end of hook. With B, YO and pull through 1 lp, *YO and pull through 2 lps; rep from * until 1 lp rem.

Tss forward pass: Insert hook from right to left behind front vertical bar, YO and pull up lp, leave lp on hook; rep from * across row.

Double-ended Tss return pass: Turn and slide sts to other end of hook. With appropriate yarn, YO and pull through 1 lp, *YO and pull through 2 lps on hook; rep from * until 1 lp rem.

Tss2tog: Insert hook behind 2 vertical bars, YO and pull up lp.

Sc BO: Insert hook from right to left behind front vertical bar, YO and pull up lp, YO and pull through 2 lps on hook; rep from * until all sts are bound off.

PATTERN STITCH
(WORKED OVER EVEN NUMBER OF STS)

See "Double-Ended Tunisian Crochet" on page 9.

Row 1: Cont with B, ch 1, *pull up lp in top strand of next horizontal bar, Tss2tog; rep from * to last horizontal bar, pull up lp in top strand of last horizontal bar. Turn and slide sts to other end. With A, work return pass.

Row 2: Cont with A, ch 1, *pull up lp in top strand of next horizontal bar, Tss2tog; rep from * to last horizontal bar, pull up lp in top strand of last horizontal bar. Turn and slide sts to other end. With B, work return pass.

Row 3: Cont with B, ch 1, pull up lp in top strand of each of the first 2 horizontal bars, Tss2tog, *pull up lp in top strand of next horizontal bar, Tss2tog; rep from * to last 2 vertical bars, pull up lp in top strand of last horizontal bar. Turn and slide sts to other end. With A, work return pass.

Row 4: Cont with A, ch 1, pull up lp in top strand of each of the first 2 horizontal bars, Tss2tog, *pull up lp in top strand of next horizontal bar, Tss2tog; rep from * to last 2 vertical bars, pull up lp in top strand of last horizontal bar. Turn and slide sts to other end. With B, work return pass.

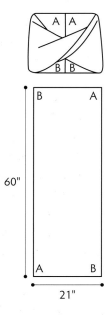

COWL

With smaller hook and A, ch 56. Switch to double-ended Tunisian crochet hook and work foundation forward pass—56 lps on hook. With B, work double-ended Tunisian crochet foundation return pass.

Work rows 1–4 for patt until piece measures approx 60" slightly stretched, ending with row 1 return pass.

Cont with A and smaller hook, sc BO.

FINISHING

Block using pin-and-mist method (page 76) before finishing. To create Mobius strip, bring BO edge to CO edge and twist 180° before seaming so that point A meets point A and point B meets point B (see diagram at left). Seam with sl-st crochet (page 74). Weave in all ends.

❦ *Design Option*

For a more classic wrap, do not seam; leave it as a rectangle. Single crochet along cast-on and bound-off edge. Wear it as a reversible shawl.

Yarn Quartet

This sporty yet chic wrap, worked with four different colors and four different stitches to create mitered rectangles, offers so many wearing options.

SKILL LEVEL

Intermediate

FINISHED MEASUREMENTS

Approx 16" x 45"

MATERIALS

Linsey from Berroco, Inc. (64% cotton, 36% linen; 1.75 oz/50g; 114 yds/105 m)

A 3 skeins in color 6552 Bluefish

B 2 skeins in color 6551 Saltwater

C 1 skein in color 6555 Pomegranate

D 3 skeins in color 6508 Chilmark

Size K-10½ (6.5 mm) Tunisian crochet hook or size required to obtain gauge

Size I-9 (5.5 mm) crochet hook or one size smaller than Tunisian crochet hook

4 removable markers or safety pins

GAUGE

12½ sts = 4" in Tss with larger hook

STITCH GUIDE

Foundation forward pass: *Insert hook in next ch, YO and pull up lp, leave lp on hook; rep from *. Do NOT turn work.

Dec return pass: YO and pull through 1 lp, (YO and pull through 2 lps) until 2 lps BEFORE marked st (fig. 1 on page 55). YO and pull through 4 lps, (YO and pull through 2 lps) until 1 lp rem (fig. 2 on page 55).

M1: Insert hook into designated space, YO and pull up lp.

Tss forward pass: *Insert hook from right to left behind front vertical bar, YO and pull up lp, leave lp on hook; rep from * across row.

Tps forward pass: *With yarn in front, insert hook from right to left behind front vertical bar, YO and pull up lp; rep from * across row.

Twisted Tss forward pass: *With hook sitting over next vertical bar, move hook from left to right,

picking up bar and twisting the hook upward, YO and pull up lp, leave lp on hook; rep from * across row.

Sc BO: *Insert hook from right to left behind front vertical bar, YO and pull up lp, YO and pull through 2 lps on hook; rep from * until all sts are bound off.

PATTERN NOTES

* *The decrease return pass creates a decrease of two stitches and is different from a standard return. See the stitch guide on page 53. The yarn over and pull through four creates a cluster of three strands. The forward pass works only the center stitch of the three-stitch cluster. See fig. 3.*

* *The garment consists of four separate miters that are joined by picking up loops from previous miter(s).*

* *See "Changing Color" on page 8.*

FIRST MITER

With smaller hook and A, ch 283. Change to Tunisian crochet hook and work foundation forward pass until 142 lps on hook, place removable marker in last

st worked, foundation forward 141—283 lps on hook (141 lps before and after marked st). Work dec return pass.

Row 1: Tps to last st, end Tss— 281 lps on hook (140 lps before and after marked st). Work dec return pass.

Row 2: Tss—279 lps on hook (139 lps before and after marked st). Work dec return pass.

Row 3: Tps to last st, Tss—277 lps on hook (138 lps before and after marked st). With B, work dec return pass.

Row 4: Tss—275 lps on hook (137 lps before and after marked st). With A, work dec return pass.

Row 5: Tps to last st, Tss—273 lps on hook (136 lps before and after marked st). With B, work dec return pass.

Row 6: Tss—271 lps on hook (135 lps before and after marked st). With A, work dec return pass.

Row 7: Cont with A, Tss—269 lps on hook (134 lps before and after marked st). With B, work dec return pass.

Row 8: Cont B, Tss—267 lps on hook (133 lps before and after marked st). With A, work dec return pass.

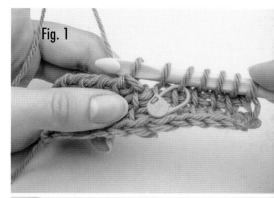
Fig. 1

Fig. 2

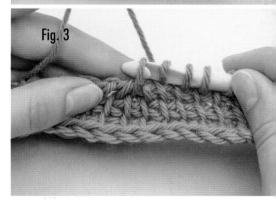
Fig. 3

Row 9: Cont with A, Tss—265 lps on hook (132 lps before and after marked st). With B, work dec return pass.

Row 10: Cont with B, Tss—263 lps on hook (131 lps before and after marked st). With A, work dec return pass.

Row 11: Cont with A, Tss—261 lps on hook (130 lps before and after marked st). With B, work dec return pass.

Row 12: Cont with B, Tss—259 lps on hook (129 lps before and after marked st). Work dec return pass.

Row 13: Twisted Tss—257 lps on hook (128 lps before and after marked st). Work dec return pass.

Row 14: Twisted Tss—255 lps on hook (127 lps before and after marked st). With A, work dec return pass.

Row 15: Cont with A, Tss—253 lps on hook (126 lps before and after marked st). With B, work dec return pass.

Row 16: Cont with B, Tss—251 lps on hook (125 lps before and after marked st). Work dec return pass.

Row 17: Twist Tss to last st, end Tss—249 lps on hook (124 lps before and after marked st). With A, work dec return pass.

Row 18: Cont with A, Tss—247 lps on hook (123 lps before and after marked st). With B, work dec return pass.

Row 19: Cont with B, Tss—245 lps on hook (122 lps before and after marked st). With A, work dec return pass.

Row 20: Cont with A, Tss—243 lps on hook (121 lps before and after marked st). Work dec return pass.

Row 21: Tps to last st, Tss—241 lps on hook (120 lps before and after marked st). Work dec return pass.

Row 22: Tss—239 lps on hook (119 lps before and after marked st). With B, work dec return pass.

Row 23: Cont with B, Tss—237 lps on hook (118 lps before and after marked st). With A, work dec return pass.

Row 24: Cont with A, Tss—235 lps on hook (117 lps before and after marked st). With B, work dec return pass.

Row 25: Cont with B, Tss—233 lps on hook (116 lps before and after marked st). With A, work dec return pass.

Row 26: Cont with A, Tss—231 lps on hook (115 lps before and after marked st). Before working the return pass, place markers for miter #2; count 21 sts from marked center st and place temporary marker. Rep for other side of central marker and place temporary marker. Work dec return pass. Cut yarn, but do NOT fasten off. Secure last lp with removable marker for later use.

SECOND MITER

Row 1: With A, beg forward pass with first marked st and work 20 sts to center marker, work center st and cont to next marker—41 sts (20 lps before and after marked st). Remove temporary markers but leave marker in center st. Work dec return pass, changing to C when 2 lps rem on hook.

Row 2: Cont with C, Tss—39 lps on hook (19 lps before and after marked st). Work dec return pass.

Row 3: (Tss, Tps) 8 times, Tss, Tss in marked st, (Tss, Tps) 8 times, Tss 2—37 lps on hook (18 lps before and after marked st). Work dec return pass.

Row 4: (Tps, Tss) 8 times, Tss in marked st, (Tss, Tps) 8 times, Tss—35 lps on hook (17 lps before and after marked st). Work dec return pass.

Row 5: (Tss, Tps) 7 times, Tss, Tss in marked st, (Tss, Tps) 7 times, Tss 2—33 lps on hook (16 lps before and after marked st). Work dec return pass.

Row 6: (Tps, Tss) 7 times, Tss in marked st, (Tss, Tps) 7 times, Tss—31 lps on hook (15 lps before and after marker). Work dec return pass.

Row 7: (Tss, Tps) 6 times, Tss, Tss in marked st (Tss, Tps) 6 times, Tss 2—29 lps on hook (14 lps before and after marked st). Work dec return pass.

Row 8: (Tps, Tss) 6 times, Tss in marked st, (Tss, TPS) 6 times, Tss—27 lps on hook (13 lps

before and after marked st). Work dec return pass.

Row 9: (Tss, Tps) 5 times, Tss, Tss in marked st, (Tss, Tps) 6 times—25 lps on hook (12 lps before and after marked st). Work dec return pass.

Row 10: (Tps, Tss) 5 times, Tss in marked st, (Tss, Tps) 5 times, Tss—23 lps on hook (11 lps before and after marked st). Work dec return pass.

Row 11: (Tss, Tps) 4 times, Tss, Tss in marked st, (Tss, Tps) 4 times, Tss 2—21 lps on hook (10 lps before and after marked st). Work dec return pass.

Row 12: (Tps, Tss) 4 times, Tss into marked st, (Tss, Tps) 4 times, Tss—19 lps on hook (9 lps before and after marked st). Work dec return pass.

Row 13: (Tss, Tps) 3 times, Tss, Tss into marked st, (Tss, Tps) 3 times, Tss 2—17 lps on hook (8 lps before and after marked st). Work dec return pass.

Row 14: (Tps, Tss) 3 times, Tss in marked st, (Tss, Tps) 3 times, Tss—15 lps on hook (7 lps before and after marked st) Work dec return pass.

Row 15: (Tss, Tps) twice, Tss, Tss in marked st, (Tss, Tps) 2 times,

Tss 2—13 lps on hook (6 lps before and after marked st). Work dec return pass.

Row 16: (Tps, Tss) twice, Tss in marked st, (Tss, Tps) twice, Tss—11 lps on hook (5 lps before and after marked st). Work dec return pass.

Row 17: Tss, Tps, Tss, Tss in marked st, Tss, Tps, Tss 2—9 lps on hook (4 lps before and after marked st). Work dec return pass.

Row 18: Tps, Tss, Tss in marked st, Tss, Tps, Tss—7 lps on hook (3 lps before and after marked st). Work dec return pass.

Row 19: Tss, Tss in marked st, Tss 2—5 lps on hook (2 lps before and after marked st). Work dec return pass.

Row 20: Tss in marked st, Tss—3 lps on hook (1 lp before and after marked st). Work dec return pass as follows: YO and pull through all lps on hook. Cut yarn and fasten off lp.

THIRD MITER

Row 1: With RS facing you and A, remove marker from last lp of miter #1 and place on hook, Tss 93, M1 in corner and mark st, work foundation forward pass along side of miter #2 (20 lps)—114 lps on hook (93 lps before marked st, 20 lps after marked st). Work dec return pass, changing to D when 2 lps remain on hook.

Row 2: Cont with D, Tss—112 lps on hook (92 lps, marked st, 19 lps). Work dec return pass.

Row 3: Twisted Tss—110 lps on hook (91 lps, marked st, 18 lps). Work dec return pass.

Row 4: Twisted Tss—108 lps on hook (90 lps, marked st, 17 lps). Work dec return pass.

Row 5: Tss—106 lps on hook (89 lps, marked st, 16 lps). Work dec return pass.

Row 6: Tps—104 lps on hook (88 lps, marked st 15 lps). Work dec return pass.

Row 7: Tss—102 lps on hook (87 lps, marked st, 14 lps). Work dec return pass.

Row 8: Twisted Tss—100 lps on hook (86 lps, marked st, 13 lps). Work dec return pass.

Row 9: Twisted Tss—98 lps on hook (85 lps, marked st, 12 lps). Work dec return pass.

Row 10: Twisted Tss—96 lps on hook (84 lps, marked st, 11 lps). Work dec return pass.

Row 11: Tss—94 lps on hook (83 lps, marked st, 10 lps). Work dec return pass.

Row 12: Twisted Tss—92 lps on hook (82 lps, marked st, 9 lps). Work dec return pass.

Row 13: Twisted Tss—90 lps on hook (81 lps, marked st, 8 lps). Work dec return pass.

Row 14: Tss—88 lps on hook (80 lps, marked st, 7 lps). Work dec return pass.

Row 15: Tps—86 lps on hook (79 lps, marked st, 6 lps). Work dec return pass.

Row 16: Tss—84 lps on hook (78 lps, marked st, 5 lps). Work dec return pass.

Row 17: Tps—82 lps on hook (77 lps, marked st, 4 lps). Work dec return pass.

Row 18: Tss—80 lps on hook (76 lps, marked st, 3 lps). Work dec return pass.

Row 19: Tps—78 lps on hook (75 lps, marked st, 2 lps). Work dec return pass.

Row 20: Tss—76 lps on hook (74 lps, marked st, 1 lp). Work dec return pass as follows: YO and pull through 4 lps, *YO and pull through 2 lps; rep from * until 1 lp rem.

With smaller hook, Sc BO.

FOURTH MITER

Row 1: With RS facing you and A, beg at last st of miter #2, work foundation forward pass over next 20 vertical bars, M1 in corner and mark lp, Tss 94—114 lps. Work dec return pass.

Rows 2–20: Work as for miter #3. Note that the number of lps on hook will be reversed.

FINISHING

With RS facing you, smaller hook, and A, beg at any corner and sc along entire edge. Cut yarn and join with duplicate st (page 73). Weave in all ends. Block using mist method (page 76).

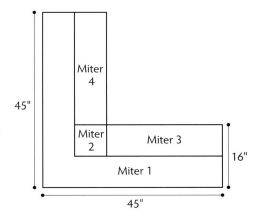

Silk Adagio

This graceful and feminine lace shawl is generously sized. The lace stitches, worked with a large hook and fine yarn, should be worked adagio (at a slow tempo) to avoid mistakes or tangles. Don't rush; just enjoy the process of creating such a delicate and exquisite shawl.

SKILL LEVEL

✦ ✦ ✦ Intermediate

FINISHED MEASUREMENTS

Approx 21½" x 76"

MATERIALS

4 skeins of Kidsilk Haze from Rowan Yarns (70% super kid mohair, 30% silk; 25 g; 229 yds/210 m) in color 00595

Size N/M-13 (9 mm) Tunisian crochet hook or size required to obtain gauge

GAUGE

12 sts = 4" in patt

STITCH GUIDE

Foundation forward pass: *Insert hook in next ch, YO and pull up lp, leave lp on hook; rep from *. Do NOT turn work.

Foundation return pass: YO, pull through 1 lp, *YO and pull through 2 lps; rep from * until 1 lp rem.

Tss forward pass: *Insert hook from right to left behind front vertical bar, YO and pull up lp, leave lp on hook; rep from * across row.

Tss return pass: YO and pull through 1 lp, *YO and pull through 2 lps; rep from * across row until 1 lp rem.

Tdc: YO, insert hook in specified stitch, YO and pull up lp, YO and pull through 2 lps, leave lp on hook.

Sc BO: *Insert hook from right to left behind front vertical bar, YO and pull up lp, YO and pull through 2 lps on hook; rep from * until all sts are bound off.

PATTERN STITCH *(MULTIPLE OF 2 STS)*

Row 1: Tss forward and return pass.

Row 2: Ch 1, *skip next vertical bar, Tdc in next vertical bar, working in front of last st made, Tdc in skipped vertical bar; rep from * to last st, Tdc in last st. Work return pass.

Row 3: Tss forward and return pass.

Rep rows 1–3 for patt.

SHAWL

Ch 64. Work foundation forward pass—64 lps on hook. Work return pass.

Work 2 rows Tss forward and return passes.

Work in patt until piece measures approx 75" slightly stretched, ending with row 3.

Work 2 rows Tss forward and return passes.

Work sc BO.

FINISHING

Weave in ends. Block using mist method (page 76) to smooth and even out sts.

Cut 4 strands of ribbon, each 20" long. Fold a single strand and apply as for fringe to each corner by inserting hook into corner st from back to front, catch folded ribbon and pull through, creating a lp. Draw ribbon ends through lp and gently pull to tighten.

Tremolo with a Twist

Encircle yourself in pure luxury with this true Mobius cowl. You don't have to be a mathematical genius; the central cast on with a half twist does the trick. Once joined, the work goes round and round, creating true Mobius with both a right-side and a wrong-side pattern per round.

SKILL LEVEL

Intermediate

FINISHED MEASUREMENTS

Approx 18" wide x 50" circumference

MATERIALS

King Baby Llama and Mulberry Silk from AslanTrends (70% king baby llama, 30% mulberry silk; 3.5 oz/100 g; 218 yds/200 m) 4

A 3 skeins in color 6036 Olive

B 1 skein in color 3089 Brick

Size L-11 (8 mm) double-ended Tunisian crochet hook or size required to obtain gauge

Size J-10 (6 mm) crochet hook or one size smaller than Tunisian crochet hook

Removable marker or safety pin

GAUGE

12 sts = 4" in Tss worked back and forth with larger hook

STITCH GUIDE

Foundation forward pass: *Insert hook in next ch, YO and pull up lp, leave lp on hook; rep from *. Do NOT turn work.

Foundation return pass: YO and pull through 1 lp, *YO and pull through 2 lps; rep from *.

Tss forward pass: *Insert hook from right to left behind front vertical bar, YO and pull up lp, leave lp on hook; rep from * across row.

Tss return pass: *YO and pull through 2 lps; rep from *.

Tps forward pass: *With yarn in front, insert hook from right to left behind front vertical bar, YO and pull up lp; rep from * across row.

Tps return pass: Work as for Tss return pass.

Sc BO: *Insert hook from right to left behind front vertical bar, YO and pull up lp, YO and pull through 2 lps on hook; rep from * until all sts are bound off.

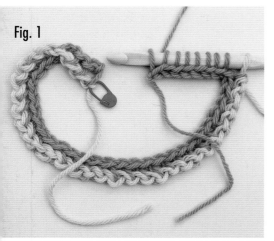

Fig. 1

Fig. 2

PATTERN STITCH *(ANY NUMBER OF STS)*

Rnd 1: With A, Tss forward pass. With B, work return pass.

Rnd 2: With A, Tps forward pass. With B, work return pass.

Rep rnds 1 and 2 for patt.

PATTERN NOTES

⁂ *This piece is worked with a double-ended crochet hook in the round as a spiral. One end of the hook is designated as the forward-pass hook and the other end is designated as the return-pass hook. Refer to "Double-Ended Tunisian Crochet" on page 9.*

⁂ *Manage your yarn after each turn to avoid frustrating tangles.*

⁂ *The Mobius join requires a central cast on where the first half foundation forward pass is worked into the back bump of the chain; then a 180° twist is given to the worked piece before beginning the second half of the foundation forward pass that is worked into a single leg of the initial chain, (fig. 1).*

⁂ *Additional rounds grow out from the center cast on as additional rounds are worked.*

COWL

With smaller hook and A, ch 152. Change to double-ended Tunisian crochet hook and work foundation forward pass into back purl bump of each ch.

Slide sts to other end of hook, make slipknot with B, place it on hook, and pull it through 1 lp. (This counts as the YO pull through 1 lp of the return pass.) Place removable st marker in st and cont with return pass, which will always be *YO and pull through 2 lps*. Stop when 8 lps rem on hook. Turn work and slide sts to forward-pass hook. Position end with removable marker to the left of forward-pass hook, twist 180° to place initial ch on top and previous foundation forward sts on the bottom.

Cont with A and foundation forward pass by inserting hook into 1 strand of each of the initial chs across. When removable marker appears in next st, the foundation forward pass is complete. Cont alternating between foundation forward pass with A and return pass with B. The central CO is complete when removable marker appears in st before forward-pass hook.

Beg rnd 1 of patt st and move marker to indicate new rnd. One complete rnd is made when marker appears in next forward st. Work rnd 2 of patt st. Once rnd 2 is completed, st marker can be removed. From this point on, beg of the rnd can easily be determined by reading the sts. When you come to Tps from previous rnd, work rnd 1 (Tss), and when you come to Tss from previous rnd, work rnd 2 (Tps).

Cont in patt until piece measures approx 7", ending with row 2. Change return-pass yarn to A. Working with 2 balls of A, 1 for forward pass and 1 for return pass, cont in patt until piece measures 18", ending with row 2.

With smaller hook and A, start sc BO after last completed forward pass, and alternate back to finish up return pass. Do NOT cut yarn. Sl st to join.

FINISHING

Cont with A and smaller hook:

Rnd 1: Ch 3, *dc 1, ch 3, skip 2 sts, dc 1 in next st; rep from * around, sl st to join.

Rnd 2: With B, *ch 3, take hook out of ch, insert hook under ch-3 lp of previous rnd, place lp back on hook; rep from * around, sl st to join (fig. 2). Fasten off last lp.

❧ *Design Option*

For a smaller cowl, cast on 76 sts and work as directed until the piece measures approximately 7", ending with row 2. Change the return pass yarn to A. Work one more forward and return pass in A, then single-crochet bind off. Only two skeins of yarn, one of each color, are required.

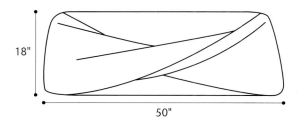

18"

50"

Duet for Hooks

Enjoy the relaxed fit of a reversible vest worked in distinctive raised vertical ribs. Worked on a double-ended hook, the reversible fabric is shown off when the lapels are folded back.

SKILL LEVEL

Intermediate

SIZES

Finished Bust Measurements: 36 (40, 44, 48)"

Finished Length: 20 (21, 22, 23)"

MATERIALS

Baby Cashmerino from Debbie Bliss (55% merino wool, 33% microfiber, 12% cashmere; 50 g; 125 m) (3)

A 2 (3, 3, 4) skeins in color 340037 (red)

B 2 (3, 3, 4) skeins in color 340058 (gray)

Size L-11 (8 mm) double-ended Tunisian crochet hook or size required to obtain gauge

Size J-10 (6 mm) crochet hook or one size smaller than Tunisian crochet hook

GAUGE

14 sts = 4" in patt st with larger hook

STITCH GUIDE

Foundation forward pass: *Insert hook in next ch, YO and pull up lp, leave lp on hook; rep from *. Do NOT turn work.

Foundation return pass: YO and pull through 1 lp, *YO and pull through 2 lps; rep from * until 1 lp rem.

Sl-st BO: *Insert hook from right to left behind front vertical bar, YO and pull through 2 lps on hook; rep from * until all sts are bound off.

PATTERN

See "Double-Ended Tunisian Crochet" on page 9.

Row 1: Forward pass with A, ch 1, *insert hook behind next vertical bar and under top strand of next horizontal bar at same time, YO and pull up lp; rep from * to last st, work as for normal edge st (insert hook behind vertical bar and strand that lies beneath it), ch 1. Slide sts to other end and with B, work return pass.

Row 2: Forward pass with B, ch 1, *insert hook behind next vertical bar and under top strand of next horizontal bar at same time, YO and pull up lp; rep from * to last st, work as for normal edge st (insert hook behind vertical bar and strand that lies beneath it), ch 1. Slide sts to other end and with A, work return pass.

Rep rows 1 and 2 for patt.

BACK

With A and smaller hook, ch 75. Change to double-ended Tunisian crochet hook and work foundation forward pass—75 lps on hook. Slide sts to other end. With B, make slipknot and place on hook, pull slipknot through 1 lp on hook, *YO and pull through 2 lps; rep from * until 1 lp rem.

Work in patt beg with row 2, and cont until piece measures approx 18 (20, 22, 24)" when slightly stretched, ending with row 2 return pass.

With A and smaller hook, sl-st BO in patt

FRONT (MAKE 2.)

With A and smaller hook, ch 70 (74, 77, 80). Change to double-ended Tunisian crochet hook and work foundation forward pass— 70 (74, 77, 80) lps on hook. Slide sts to other end. With B, make slipknot and place on hook, pull slipknot through 1 lp on hook, *YO and pull through 2 lps; rep from * until 1 lp rem.

Work in patt beg with row 2, and cont until piece measures approx 9 (10, 11, 12)" when slightly stretched, ending with row 2.

With A and smaller hook, sl-st BO in patt.

FINISHING

Mark shoulder seams by measuring from side across top back for 6 (6½, 7, 8)". Place RS tog and sl-st crochet (page 74) shoulder seams. Mark armhole opening by measuring 8 (8½, 9, 9½)" down side from shoulder seam. Mark 2" from bottom for side slit. With RS tog, sl-st crochet side seams between markers.

Weave in all ends. Block using pin-and-mist method (page 76).

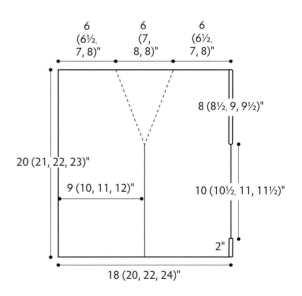

Grace Note

So versatile, so textured, so stylish—it's the must-have cardigan of the season. This roomy short-sleeved V-neck sweater will go with everything and you'll want to take it everywhere. The grace note is the decorative pineapple-crochet edge.

SKILL LEVEL

░░░ ░░░ ░░░ ░░░ Experienced

SIZES

Finished Bust Measurement: 40½ (42½, 48, 54½)" excluding crochet edge

Finished Length: 21 (22, 23½, 25)"

MATERIALS

9 (10, 11, 12) skeins of Cotton Ball from Claudia Hand Painted Yarns (100% cotton; 50 g; 130 yds) in color Just Plum

Size L-11 (8 mm) Tunisian crochet hook or size required to obtain gauge

Size J-10 (6 mm) crochet hook or one size smaller than Tunisian crochet hook

Stick pin (optional)

GAUGE

12 sts = 4" in patt with larger hook

STITCH GUIDE

Foundation forward pass: *Insert hook in next ch, YO and pull up lp, leave lp on hook; rep from *. Do NOT turn work.

Foundation return pass: YO and pull through 1 lp, *YO and pull through 2 lps; rep from * until 1 lp rem.

Tss forward pass: *Insert hook from right to left behind front vertical bar, YO and pull up lp, leave lp on hook; rep from * across row.

Tss return pass: YO and pull through 1 lp, *YO and pull through 2 lps; rep from * across row until 1 lp rem.

FPTs forward pass: *Insert hook between sts around both vertical bars, YO and pull up lp and leave lp on hook; rep from * to last st, Tss. See photo on page 72.

Tfc forward pass: *Ch 2, insert hook in second ch from hook, and pull up lp; rep from * for specified number of sts.

M1h: Insert hook between horizontal strands, YO and pull up lp.

Sc BO: *Insert hook from right to left behind front vertical bar, YO and pull up lp, YO and pull up 2 lps on hook; rep from * until all sts are bound off.

PATTERN

Row 1: Tss forward and return pass.

Row 2: FPTs forward pass to last st, Tss. Work Tss return pass.

Rep rows 1 and 2 for patt.

PATTERN NOTE

Both fronts and back are worked separately from the neck down and joined at the underarm.

BACK

With smaller hook, ch 48 (52, 54, 60). Change to Tunisian crochet hook and foundation forward pass—48 (52, 54, 60) lps on hook. Work return pass.

Work in patt until piece measures 8 (8, 8½, 9)", ending with row 2 return pass. Do NOT BO, but fasten off last st and cut yarn.

LEFT FRONT

With smaller hook, ch 15 (17, 17, 19). Change to Tunisian crochet hook and foundation forward pass—15 (17, 17, 19) lps on hook. Work return pass.

Work 4 rows in patt.

Cont in patt and AT THE SAME TIME inc at neck edge on EOR 11 (11, 12, 13) times as follows: M1h, work in patt across row—26 (28, 29, 32) lps on hook. Work return pass.

Cont in patt until piece measures 8 (8, 8½, 9)", ending with row 2. Do NOT BO, but fasten off last st and cut yarn.

RIGHT FRONT

With smaller hook, ch 15 (17, 17, 19). Change to Tunisian crochet hook and foundation forward pass—15 (17, 17, 19) lps on hook. Work return pass.

Work 4 rows in patt.

Cont in patt and AT THE SAME TIME inc at neck edge on EOR 11 (11, 12, 13) times as follows: M1h, work in patt across to last st, work last st.

Cont in patt until piece measures 8 (8, 8½, 9)", ending with row 2 return pass—26 (28, 29, 32) lps on hook. Work return pass.

JOIN BACK AND FRONTS

Work row 1 of patt across right front—26 (28, 29, 32) lps on hook, Tfc 10 (12, 16, 16)—[36 (40, 45, 48) lps on hook], work in patt across back, Tfc 10 (12, 16, 16), work in patt across left front—126 (132, 148, 168) lps on hook. Work return pass.

Cont in patt until piece measures 13 (14, 15, 16)" from underarm join.

With smaller hook, sc BO.

SLEEVE (MAKE 2.)

With smaller hook, ch 48 (48, 52, 54). Change to Tunisian crochet hook and work foundation forward pass—48 (48, 52, 54) lps on hook. Work foundation return pass.

Work in patt until piece measures 5 (5, 6, 7)", ending with row 2 return pass.

With smaller hook, sc BO.

FINISHING

Block using pin-and-mist method (page 76) to smooth and even out sts.

With RS tog, sl-st crochet (page 74) shoulder seams, sleeves to body, and underarm seams.

With RS facing you, smaller hook, and beg at bottom-right front, work pineapple-crochet edge along right front, neck, left front, and around bottom edges as follows:

Row 1: Sc along edge, working 2 sc into each corner st.

Row 2: Ch 2, *hdc, (YO, insert hook in space to right of hdc, pull up lp) 3 times (7 lps on hook), YO and pull through 7 lps on hook (pineapple made), ch 1, sk next sc; rep from * around edge, working 2 pineapples without skipping st in corner. Sl st to join.

Row 3: Sc around edge. Fasten off yarn and join with duplicate st (page 73).

Weave in all ends. Block again using mist method (page 76) to smooth seams and edging.

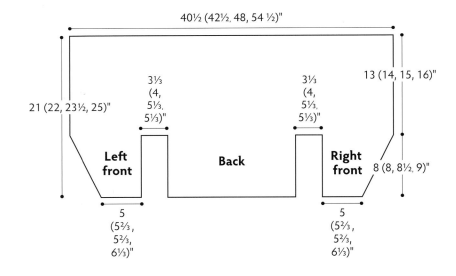

Front-post Tunisian forward pass

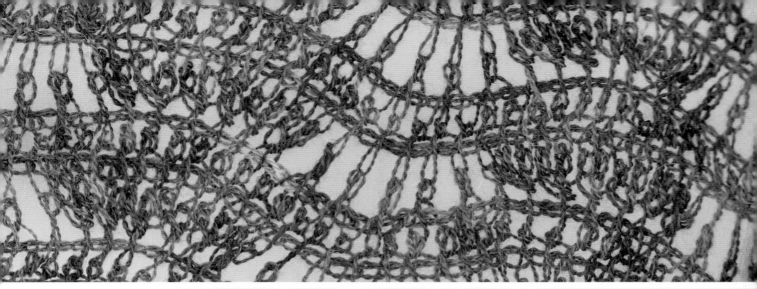

Coda

Good finishing makes the difference between a professional-looking piece of work and one that looks homemade. Here are some of the basic techniques necessary to give your work a fine, tailored look.

JOINING A NEW BALL OF YARN

A great finish begins long before the end is in sight. Whenever possible, attach a new ball of yarn at the beginning of the row. Place the end of the yarn over the hook and begin to work. If you prefer to anchor your yarn, tie the new strand onto the old tail with a single knot. Slide the new knot up the old tail to the needle and begin working with the new yarn.

JOIN WITH DUPLICATE STITCH

Based on the duplicate stitch used in knitting, this method of joining give a smooth and bump-less join. After working the final round, fasten off the stitch and thread the tail through a tapestry needle. Insert the needle from front to back under the back leg of the first stitch of the round. Insert the tail into the back of the last stitch of the round. Weave in end.

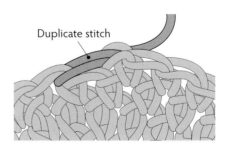

Duplicate stitch

SEAMING

A few of the projects require seaming, and there are several methods suited to Tunisian crochet. Regardless of the method you prefer, seams should be smooth and not easily detected.

Whipstitch gives a flat and durable seam. Align edges with right sides together and wrong sides facing you. Using a tapestry needle, take the needle from front to back through both layers of fabric, keeping the front and back corresponding stitches together. Repeat across the edge.

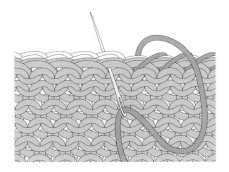

Slip-stitch crochet gives a flexible yet stable seam. Align edges with right sides together for an inside ridge, or wrong sides together for an outside ridge. Use the same size crochet hook used to make the beginning chain. Insert the hook through the stitch on both layers, yarn over hook, and pull through both layers and through the loop on the hook. Repeat across the edge.

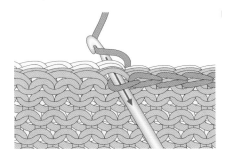

EDGES

Tunisian crochet usually requires a crocheted edge to help the edges lie flat and give the piece of work a better finish. Generally a smaller hook size is used for the edge than the size used for the body of the work. A round of single crochet (sc) is worked as the first round and serves as a foundation row for additional rounds. When working into a corner stitch, two or three stitches are worked into the same stitch to create the curve of the corner. A crocheted edge is also an easy way to create buttonhole loops.

Single Crochet (sc)

To work, insert the hook into next stitch, yarn over hook and pull up a loop (two loops on hook), yarn over hook and pull through two loops.

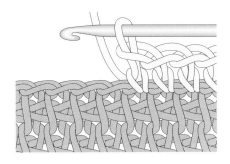

Half Double Crochet (hdc)

To work, yarn over hook, insert hook into stitch, yarn over hook and pull through loop (three loops on hook), yarn over hook and pull through three loops.

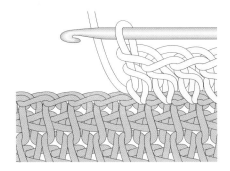

Double Crochet (dc)

To work, yarn over hook, insert the hook into next stitch, yarn over hook and pull up a loop (three loops on hook), yarn over hook and pull through two loops (two loops remaining), yarn over hook and pull through two loops.

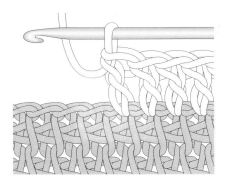

Reverse Single Crochet (rev sc)

Also known as shrimp or crab stitch, this is a single crochet that is worked in reverse—that is, left to right. To work, insert the hook into the next stitch on the right, yarn over hook and pull up a loop (two loops on hook), yarn over hook and pull through two loops.

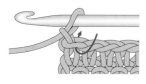

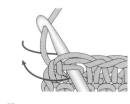

WEAVING IN ENDS

Thread a tapestry needle and weave the yarn through three or four stitches on the wrong side of the work. Check the right side to be sure the stitches are not showing before clipping yarn.

BLOCKING

Blocking is the final process of adjusting the contour of your piece to its proper proportions, and evens the stitches into a uniform shape. Blocking is done either before assembly so that all pieces are shaped to their finished measurements and fit together easily, or after all seams are completed and the ends woven in.

Some pieces require more blocking than others; the yarn fiber content and weight along with the stitch pattern will influence the amount of blocking a piece requires. Natural fibers such as wool respond well to blocking, while synthetic fibers respond very little. Lace requires blocking to open up the stitches and reveal the beautiful lace pattern.

First choose a flat, waterproof surface to spread out the piece to be blocked. Blocking boards can be purchased, or you can improvise: the top on an ironing board works for smaller pieces, or the floor covered with a towel will work. Regardless of the method used for blocking, the piece should remain in place until dry.

Mist Method

Lay the knitted piece on the surface, shaping to specified dimensions. Fill a clean spray bottle with water and mist lightly with water. Allow to dry completely before moving.

Pin-and-Mist Method

Lay the knitted piece on the surface and pin the piece to specified measurements. Fill a clean spray bottle with water and mist heavily with water. Allow to dry completely before removing pins.

Abbreviations

approx	approximately		PU	pick up
beg	begin(ning)		rem	remain(ing)(s)
BO	bind off		rep(s)	repeat(s)
ch(s)	chain(s) or chain stitch(es)		rnd(s)	round(s)
ch-	refers to chain, or chain space previously made, such as "ch-1 space"		RS	right side
CO	cast on		sc	single crochet(s)
cont	continue(ing)(s)		sk	skip
dc	double crochet(s)		sl 1	slip one stitch
dec(s)	decrease(ing)(s)		sl st(s)	slip stitch(es)
ExTks	extended Tunisian knit stitch (page 41)		sp(s)	space(s)
ExTss	extended Tunisian simple stitch (page 17)		st(s)	stitch(es)
FPTs	front post Tunisian stitch (page 69)		tog	together
g	gram(s)		Tdc	Tunisian double crochet (page 47)
hdc	half double crochet(s)		Tdc2tog	work 2 Tdc together—1 st decreased (page 47)
inc(s)	increase(ing)(s)		Tfc	Tunisian foundation crochet (page 69)
lp(s)	loop(s)		Tks	Tunisian knit stitch (page 7)
m	meter(s)		Tps	Tunisian purl stitch (page 8)
mm	millimeter(s)		Tss	Tunisian simple stitch (page 7)
M1	make 1 stitch between vertical bars—1 stitch increased (page 53)		Tss2tog	work 2 Tss together—1 stitch decreased (page 37)
M1h	make 1 stitch between horizontal bars—1 stitch increased (page 71)		Tts	Tunisian triple stitch (page 27)
oz	ounce(s)		WS	wrong side
patt(s)	pattern(s)		yd(s)	yard(s)
			YO(s)	yarn over(s)

Useful Information

Yards x .91 = meters	Meters x 1.09 = yards	Grams x .035 = ounces	Ounces x 28.35 = grams

STANDARD YARN WEIGHTS

Yarn-Weight Symbol and Category Name	0 Lace	1 Super Fine	2 Fine	3 Light	4 Medium	5 Bulky
Types of Yarn in Category	Fingering, 10-count crochet thread	Sock, Fingering, Baby	Sport, Baby	DK, Light Worsted	Worsted, Afghan, Aran	Chunky, Craft, Rug
Crochet Gauge* Range in Single Crochet to 4"	32 to 42 sts**	21 to 32 sts	16 to 20 sts	12 to 17 sts	11 to 14 sts	8 to 11 sts
Recommended Hook in Metric Size Range	2.25 mm	2.25 to 3.5 mm	3.5 to 4.5 mm	4.5 to 5.5 mm	5.5 to 6.5 mm	6.5 to 9 mm
Recommended Hook in US Size Range	B-1	B-1 to E-4	E-4 to 7	7 to I-9	I-9 to K-10½	K-10½ to M-13

*These are guidelines only. The above reflect the most commonly used gauges and needle or hook sizes for specific yarn categories.

**Lace-weight yarns are usually knit or crocheted on larger needles and hooks to create lacy, openwork patterns. Accordingly, a gauge range is difficult to determine. Always follow the gauge stated in your pattern.

CROCHET HOOK SIZES

Tunisian hooks are available in the following sizes.

Millimeter	US Size*
3.75 mm	F-5
4 mm	G-6
4.5 mm	7
5 mm	H-8
5.5 mm	I-9
6 mm	J-10
6.5 mm	K-10½
8 mm	L-11
9 mm	M/N-13
10 mm	N/P-15
12 mm	O-17
15 mm	P/Q
16 mm	Q-19
19 mm	S-35
22 mm	T-42
25 mm	U-50

Letter or number may vary. Rely on the millimeter sizing.

SKILL LEVELS

※ **Beginner:** Projects for first-time crocheters using basic stitches; minimal shaping.

※ ※ **Easy:** Projects using yarn with basic stitches, repetitive stitch patterns, simple color changes, and simple shaping and finishing.

※ ※ ※ **Intermediate:** Projects using a variety of techniques, such as basic lace patterns or color patterns; midlevel shaping and finishing.

※ ※ ※ ※ **Experienced:** Projects with intricate stitch patterns, techniques, and dimension, such as nonrepeating patterns, multicolor techniques, fine threads, small hooks, detailed shaping, and refined finishing.

Resources

Contact the following companies to locate the yarns and supplies used in this book.

Araucania
www.knittingfever.com
Lauca

Artemis
www.artemisinc.com
Hanah Silk Ribbon

AslanTrends
www.aslantrends.com
King Baby Llama and Mulberry Silk

Berroco, Inc.
www.berroco.com
Linsey

Blue Sky Alpacas
www.blueskyalpacas.com
Alpaca Silk

Brown Sheep Company, Inc.
www.brownsheep.com
Lanaloft Bulky

Classic Elite Yarns
www.classiceliteyarns.com
Soft Linen

Claudia Hand Painted Yarns
www.claudiaco.com
Cotton Ball

Debbie Bliss
www.knittingfever.com
Baby Cashmerino

Denise Interchangeable Knitting and
Crochet Hooks
www.knitdenise.com
Hooks

Filatura Di Crosa
www.tahkistacycharles.com
Tempo

Interlacements
www.interlacementsyarns.com
New York 200

Jade Sapphire Exotic Fibres
www.jadesapphire.com
Silk/Cashmere

Lantern Moon
www.lanternmoon.com
Scrumptious

Madelinetosh
www.madelinetosh.com
Tosh Merino Light

Misti Alpaca
www.mistialpaca.com
Hand Paint Lace

Mountain Colors
www.mountaincolors.com
Merino Ribbon

Rowan Yarns
www.knitrowan.com
Kidsilk Haze

SweetGeorgia Yarns
www.sweetgeorgiayarns.com
Tough Love Sock

Acknowledgments

Thanks to all who attended my classes. Your suggestions, questions, requests, and in some cases even demands, have sparked my creativity.

Chris and Ellie, a special thank-you to both of you for sharing your musical expertise and your great sense of humor.

Thank you Ruth and Ursula for bravely picking up your hooks even as the patterns were being revised.

To all the talented dynamos at Martingale, I extend my sincere appreciation for all you do.

And last but not least, love and thanks to my husband, Kevin.